Baptists *and Their* Contribution *to the* Shaping *of* Jesus

Edgar V. McKnight

© 2013

Published in the United States by Nurturing Faith Inc., Macon GA, www.nurturingfaith.net.

Library of Congress Cataloging-in-Publication Data is available.

ISBN 978-1-938514-20-3

All rights reserved. Printed in the United States of America

CONTENTS

Prologue
The Baptist Vision
Persistent Questions about Christ
v

Chapter 1
The Contribution of General and Particular Baptists
Shaping the Free-Church Congregations
1

Chapter 2
Jesus as "Christ" and "Lord"
New Testament Confessions and Hymns
11

Chapter 3
"Truly God" and "Truly Man"
The Church's Search for Orthodoxy
21

Chapter 4
Southern Baptists Defending the Faith
Crawford H. Toy, Basil Manly, Jr., and A. T. Robertson
29

Chapter 5
Southern Baptists Valuing Historical Criticism
John A. Broadus and A. T. Robertson
37

Chapter 6
Northern Baptists and a New Era among Baptists
William Newton Clarke
47

Chapter 7
Northern Baptists and the Advocacy of Modernism
Shailer Mathews
57

Chapter 8
Northern Baptists and a New Historical Appreciation of Jesus
Shirley Jackson Case
65

Chapter 9
How Much of a Man Was Jesus Christ?
A Christological Controversy in England
75

Chapter 10
Jesus and/as Parable of God
Constructing a Faith Image of Jesus
85

PROLOGUE

The Baptist Vision

Persistent Questions about Christ

Christians in general have understood and shaped Jesus in different fashion with different results. They have shaped Jesus with metaphysical and theological speculation and affirmation, through historical-critical investigation and judgment, and by artistic and literary imagination. One particular way of shaping Jesus does not validate or invalidate other ways of shaping Jesus. Different shapings allowed different ways of mapping Jesus to the world, different ways of mapping human experience to the divine, and different ways of confessing Jesus as Lord. In these different shapings Jesus may become a parable of God, an iconic representation of God as the divine is experienced in the story of Jesus, the teaching of Jesus, and the claims made in the name of Jesus.

This prologue provides a framework for understanding the peculiar way Baptists and free-church Christians have contributed to the understanding of Jesus as the Christ. What contribution to thought about Jesus is offered today by the Baptist vision and the Baptist answer to persistent questions about the identity of Jesus Christ? The Baptist vision provides a focus and gives a distinct flavor to the dynamic Baptist contribution to the shaping of Jesus.

The study has a historical focus going back to the earliest Baptists in England four centuries ago. But it has a contemporary focus also, suggesting satisfying ways of mapping *our* story of Jesus to *our* story of God. In this satisfying mapping, contemporary and ancient understanding of Jesus' humanity and divinity are correlated. Jesus is mapped in terms of our understanding of God, and our understanding of God is mapped in terms of Jesus.

Five interrelated elements are a part of the total Baptist vision according to the Baptist theologian James Wm. McClendon. These elements are biblicism, mission, liberty, discipleship, and community.

> Biblicism . . . understood . . . as humble acceptance of the authority of Scripture for both faith and practice . . . Mission (or evangelism), understood . . . as the responsibility of witness to Christ . . . Liberty, or soul competency, understood as the God-given freedom to respond to God without the intervention of the state or other powers . . . Discipleship, understood . . . as life transformed into service by the lordship of Jesus Christ . . . Community, understood . . . as sharing together in a storied life of obedient service to and with Christ.[1]

These emphases may be seen in Baptist life beginning with the earliest Baptist congregations in England and extending to modern-day Baptist groups throughout the world. Central for the various forms and expressions of Baptist life is "believing in Jesus." Emphasis upon personal experience and relationship plays a vital part for Baptists in the mapping from the Jesus of the Gospels and his disciples to the life of the believer and the mapping from Jesus to the being of God.

The Baptist vision and emphasis on believing in Jesus may be correlated with the Baptist take on both the classical two natures model and the more contemporary historical model of Christology. In the church during the classical period of the shaping of Jesus Christ (the two natures model), the divinity of Jesus was basic and the emphasis was on the way the divine could become human without a diminution of the divine. The two natures model of Christology focused not upon mapping from the human to the divine but upon mapping from the divine to the human. Christologies founded on this model were always in danger of docetism (from the Greek word *dokeō*, to seem)—a view that Jesus only *seemed* to be human. The intellectual tools used in the two natures model allow and validate a Jesus who is divine but whose humanity is problematic. The historical model of Christology, on the other hand, asks how movement may be made from the human to the divine. The historical elements of the story of Jesus provide assistance in shaping a Jesus worthy of discipleship. When the historical elements are emphasized, however, there is always the tendency toward Unitarianism (Socinianism).

In his helpful analysis of the distinct values of historical Christology in relation to the two natures model of Christology, McClendon moves from the models themselves to the underlying and persistent questions faced by Christian thinkers throughout all of the changes in Christological thought. These questions and their answers provide a template against which we can appreciate the Baptist contribution to Christological thought. The first question grows out of the presumptuous or even blasphemous nature of intersecting the identity of Jesus with the identity of God. McClendon poses the question in moral terms: "[W]hat right has Jesus Christ to absolute lordship—the lordship that scripture assigns to God alone?"[2] A satisfactory answer is necessary to guard against faithfulness to Christ being necessarily fanatical or necessarily limited.

The second question is related to the first. It asks how we can answer the first question and intersect the identity of Jesus with the identity of God without offending the teaching of monotheism that God alone is God. How can those who believe in one God tell the Jesus story as their own.

The third question has to do with the uniqueness of Jesus' human life and its relation to the lives of others. What does the full humanity of Jesus of Nazareth imply about the spiritual possibilities of human life in general? Can Jesus' kind of life be ours also? An answer may take one of two divergent paths. It can hold that in contrast to all others who share human nature, Jesus' unique relation to God issued in a life that was both unsurpassable and unapproachable. This expresses the reverence that Christians feel for the earthly life of their Lord. Contrariwise, an answer can hold that exactly because of Jesus' unique relation to God he entered upon a road that each of us must travel. That seems to express well the appeal to discipleship in the Gospels. In summary fashion, McClendon poses the third question: "[H]ow Christlike, how like the Master, are disciples' lives to be?"[3]

The two natures model affirmed a transcendental ground for Christ's lordship (question one). But, according to McClendon, it violated even ancient rationality and seemed indifferent to concern for the Jesus story as a viable model of conduct for disciples.[4] The historical model makes historical research the seat of authority. But by definition, historical research is unable to answer the first question. In reaction to the introduction of historical criticism, Gotthold Ephraim Lessing posited the challenge of historical study to faith in his perception of a "wide, ugly ditch" between the "accidental truths of history" and the "necessary truths of reason."[5] Historical study places humankind in a system of ceaseless change on the historical level. This is in absolute contrast to the biblico-theological view of late antiquity. Historical research, however, has provided a very successful way of answering the third question as to how Christlike disciples' lives are to be. The historical model (citing McClendon's summary of Donald Baillie's assessment of "the harvest of liberal theology") brought a new appreciation of the human Jesus, so that . . .

> [I]t seemed to students they were as near as yesterday to the one who walked and taught in Galilee and Judaea. For them this entailed the full humanity of Jesus' personal existence—a human body, a human mind, a human self. These in turn entailed the humanity of his psychic makeup . . . His knowledge was limited. The insights he displayed were fully human insights; his emotions were human emotions; his moral life developed as do human moral lives; his temptations were real temptations; his faith was human faith; the miracles or signs he worked were done with human faith, and he said the disciples would do even more than he.[6]

Although the historical model in and of itself left much to be desired, we can only celebrate its real gains: "It brought the confession of Christ's humanity into its own day."[7]

The story of the development among Baptists of historical and critical approaches to the study of the Bible and to the confession of Jesus is not simply an account of activities in a particular place and period in intellectual and cultural history. It is a story with contemporary relevance. The Baptist tradition supports a shaping of Jesus Christ in line with the two natures model of the ancient creeds. But the historical approach to the Bible in general and to Jesus of Nazareth in particular challenges a simplistic affirmation of those creeds. How did a voice for historical-critical approaches develop and continue to be heard in a denominational tradition that historically valued the authority of Scripture, the piety of Christian experience, and the supernatural nature of faith? The resources and tools that have been developed and used in the Baptist shaping of Jesus may be related to developments in philosophy, theology, and social thought, to be sure. But the history of Christological shaping by Baptists is not just a series of responses to those developments. The shaping of Jesus is not simply an intellectual exercise. It is a creative effort to relate God's Word to the world. And this must be the criterion for the validation of the different shapings in the story of Baptists.

In the following pages we will examine the shaping of Jesus, beginning with a chapter that introduces the origins of modern Baptists in England in the beginning of the seventeenth century and compares and contrasts those early "sects" (General Baptists and Particular Baptists) with the "church" (the Church of England), and the Jesus shaped by those Baptist sects is compared with the sacramental shaping of Jesus by the Church of England. The number and nature of the sacraments distinguish Baptists from the Roman Catholic Church and the Church of England. For Catholics the seven sacraments of the church (Baptism, Eucharist, Confirmation, Holy Orders, Penance, Extreme Unction, and Matrimony) are salvific-conveying events. For Baptists the two ordinances (not sacraments) of baptism and the Lord's Supper are outward signs or symbols of a salvation previously effected.

Following an examination of how General Baptists and Particular Baptists shaped the church, two chapters are devoted to the resources drawn upon by early Baptists and other Christians for their shaping of Jesus: the New Testament witness to Jesus and the two natures model of the early creeds. The difference between today and the function and ambience of the New Testament and early creeds cautions us against a credulous and literal appropriation of the divine titles and attributes found helpful by the early church.

In chapters four through eight, the historical revolution in Jesus studies and in Christological argumentation among Baptists is introduced and given detailed treatment in a discussion of "seminal" figures in Southern Baptist and American (Northern) Baptist scholarship. These seminal figures include the Southern Baptists John A. Broadus and A. T. Robertson and the Northern (American) Baptists William Newton Clarke, Shailer Mathews, and Shirley Jackson Case. Different ways of relating the new historical learning (higher criticism) to the faith are examined—namely, evangelicalism, liberalism, modernism, conservative evangelicalism, strict conservatism, and fundamentalism—with a dramatic challenge to inherited orthodoxy on the part of Southern Baptists as well as Northern (American) Baptists.

A chapter on the Christological controversy of the early 1970s in England provides an opportunity to appreciate both the attempt to restate the position of the classical creeds in contemporary language and the spirited defense of the biblical witness to and contemporary relevance of incarnational language. A final chapter argues that the language and religious argumentation relating Jesus to the divine may be seen as parabolic. It requires readers and hearers to find and complete the meaning. The kind of knowledge involved in this transactive process is not only historical knowledge (authenticated by historical-critical tools and approaches) but also historic and faith knowledge. The result of this transactive relationship is that God is experienced in Jesus Christ. The earliest disciples experienced God in Jesus Christ, and the witness they gave to this experience and meaning is capable of engendering the same experience today. This experience of God enables contemporary validation of the ancient understanding and testimony of incarnation.

Notes

[1] James Wm. McClendon, *Ethics, Systematic Theology*, vol. 1 (Nashville: Abingdon Press, 1986) 28.
[2] ———, *Doctrine, Systematic Theology*, vol. 2 (Nashville: Abingdon, 1994) 194.
[3] Ibid., 195.
[4] Ibid., 256.
[5] Ibid., 257.
[6] Ibid., 262.
[7] Ibid., 263.

CHAPTER 1

The Contribution of General and Particular Baptists
Shaping the Free-Church Congregations

Modern Baptists go back to the early 1600s with the formation of General and Particular Baptist congregations in England. The titles "general" and "particular" come from the perspectives taken on atonement.

General Baptists believed in a "general" atonement; that is, anyone who believes in Christ can be saved. They were influenced by the Dutch theologian Jacob Arminius, and like other Arminians General Baptists also believed in the possibility of falling from grace and gave more attention to associations of congregations, with limited autonomy of any specific congregation. The earliest General Baptist church was formed in 1609 with John Smyth and Thomas Helwys as the two primary founders.

By the late 1630s, Particular Baptists surfaced. They were influenced by John Calvin and believed that God had elected some to salvation and that the elect could not lose their salvation. The name "particular" comes from the teaching that Christ died not for all humankind but for "particular ones" elected by God.

Early Baptist Congregations in England

The story of early Baptists and their understanding of Jesus is a part of the larger story of the church in Europe in general and in England in particular. By the time Baptist congregations were formed, the major Protestant bodies such as the Lutheran, Reformed, and Anglican churches had already come into existence. The Bible had been put into the languages of the people, and major religious figures were influential through their preaching—Martin Luther, Ulrich Zwingli, John Calvin, Conrad Grebel, and others. The Renaissance had brought a widespread and growing enlightenment.

Reform was in the air. Baptist shaping of Jesus, then, was inspired by broad religious developments in conjunction with the way Baptists did church.

Puritanism and Separatism in England directly influenced the origins of Baptists. A growing number of churchmen in the sixteenth century advocated a "pure" church, and a "puritan" party arose. The aim of Puritans was a reform of church—not a break with the Church of England. They wanted simplification of worship patterns, modification of church polity from episcopal to presbyterial, and the adoption of doctrines that were more Calvinistic. The Puritans were not successful in their attempt to reform. The next step, then, was separation from the Church of England. Some saw separation as a pragmatic move, with the idea that a temporary separation might encourage reform. Others saw separation in terms of principle. They were convinced that the church in principle should be free of government connections

By the 1550s, groups of separatists came to be evident in England. They began to meet independently of the Church of England for worship, Bible reading, and prayer. The well-known letter of Bishop Grindal to Henry Bullinger, dated in London June 9, 1568, gives evidence of early separatism:

> Some London citizens of the lowest order, together with four or five ministers, remarkable neither for their judgment nor learning, have openly separated from us; and sometimes in private homes, sometimes in the fields, and occasionally even in ships, they have held their meetings and administered the sacraments. Besides this, they have ordained ministers, elders, and deacons, after their own way.[1]

The earliest Baptist congregation resulted from a group of separatists who met in Gainsborough in the Midlands. John Smyth was the major figure in the development of this church. The Baptist historian H. Leon McBeth said that Smyth was a "remarkable man . . . a capable theologian and writer":

> Apparently, Smyth entered Christ's College, Cambridge University, in 1586 to prepare for the ministry. After graduation in 1590 he was invited to remain as a fellow at Christ's College and served for a time as a teacher there. He was ordained an Anglican priest by the Bishop of London in 1594. Smyth was greatly influenced by a teacher at Cambridge,

Francis Johnson, who later led a Separatist congregation
... One record shows he was in the "clink," a well-known
English prison, for a time for his refusal to conform to the
teachings and practices of the Church of England ... Not
a man to compromise, Smyth often used strong language
in his criticisms. He considered many Anglican priests as
"too papist" (i.e., too much like Catholicism); infant baptism he equated with spiritual adultery; and he was known
to rebuke prominent sinners by name from the pulpit.[2]

Smyth progressed through the stages of Anglicanism, Puritanism, and Separatism. It was in Gainsborough that he broke completely with the Church of England and was accepted as minister of the Separatist congregation. Other leaders in the congregation were the ministers John Robinson, William Brewster, and William Bradford, and the well-to-do layman Thomas Helwys—who was educated in law at Gray's Inn, London. McBeth said, "If Smyth was the more dynamic and creative, Helwys made his contribution in clarity of thought and stability of action."[3]

When the group grew so large that it became visible to outsiders as a distinct congregation, it was split into two groups: a Robinson-Bradford group and a Smyth-Helwys group. Both of these groups along with other groups migrated to Holland as religious refugees about the same time at the turn of the seventeenth century.

The Smyth-Helwys congregants were not marked by Baptist distinctives when they migrated to Amsterdam. At first they were in fellowship with a group called "The Ancient Church," most of the members of which had migrated to Amsterdam in 1593. When the congregants left England in 1607, they were not Baptist. They formed a church on the basis of the Old Testament covenant principle, made no provision for believer's baptism, and allowed a degree of government control of religion. But by 1609 they changed on all these points and Smyth founded a church on the basis of the baptism of believers.

The question of the baptism of the members of the church is most interesting since none of the members had experienced believer's baptism but rather had been baptized as infants under the authorization of the Church of England. Smyth solved the problem by baptizing himself using the form of affusion or pouring, and then baptizing Helwys, and then about forty others.

Shortly, however (perhaps within months), Smyth came to the view that his self-baptism was not proper, that true baptism could be performed only by someone who had been properly baptized. Smyth then repudiated his baptism and asked the church members to repudiate their baptism. The proper baptism that Smyth now advocated was that of the Mennonites. Some of the church members refused to follow the changes advocated by Smyth, including Helwys and a small number of members of the congregation who excluded Smyth and more than twenty of his followers. These excluded individuals were received into Mennonite fellowship on January 21, 1615. By this time Smyth had died, and so Smyth himself was not received into Mennonite fellowship during his lifetime.

Smyth recovered believer's baptism, but it was the Helwys group that continued Baptist beginnings. The Helwys group remained faithful to Baptist principles as is seen by a confession drawn up in 1611. The Helwys followers baptized believers only (although not yet by immersion), made room for free will and falling from grace, and allowed each congregation to elect its own officers. This group returned to England, and at least five General Baptist churches were established in England by 1624. By 1650 at least forty-seven such churches existed.

The group that would give rise to the earliest Particular Baptist congregation was "gathered" in 1616 in the Southwark section of London by Henry Jacob. Jacob had earlier called for reform in the Church of England, been jailed for his views (even though his views were much more moderate than those of John Smyth), went into exile in Holland where he served as pastor of an independent church near Leyden, and returned to England where he gathered the church in London. In 1624 John Lathrop assumed pastorate of the Southwark church, about two years after Jacob had moved to Virginia. During Lathrop's pastorate several individuals of pronounced separatist convictions joined the church, and in 1630 some members withdrew because their strict views were not acceptable to the majority. Further schism followed in 1633.

In 1634 Lathrop left the pastorate of the Southwark congregation, and Henry Jessey became pastor in 1637. Jessey attempted to follow the tolerant principles of Jacob, but internal strife continued. In 1638 six additional members left the church over the question of baptism of believers. They were said to be "of the same judgment with Samuel Eaton" about baptism, and the records show that the six joined with a Mr. Spilsbury. What all of this means is open to question. Spilsbury may have succeeded Eaton as pastor of the 1633 group or he may have headed another separatist church that had adopted believer's baptism in 1638. Historians judge that definitely by 1638 and possibly by 1633 a Particular Baptist church was formed in London. Evidence exists of the formation of another Particular Baptist Church in 1639, and by 1644 seven Particular Baptist churches in or near London issued a joint confession of faith.

English Baptists recovered biblical baptism in two stages. First they judged that baptism applies not to infants but to believers. General Baptists taught this as early as 1609 and Particular Baptists by 1638 or earlier. The second step was to restore the ancient mode of baptism by immersion. Particular Baptists were the first to adopt this mode, definitely practicing immersion beginning in 1640-41. General Baptists certainly practiced immersion by 1660 and probably as early as mid-century.

Church and Sect

In the early seventeenth century Baptists rediscovered distinctive evangelical doctrines such as salvation by grace through faith, a "gathered church," believer's baptism, the authority of scripture, and religious liberty. These were not invented in the seventeenth century, but they were articulated afresh in a new era. We obtain some help in seeing the significance of the Baptist shaping of Jesus over against the sacramental shaping by following the typology suggested by Ernst Troeltsch, a German theologian of the early twentieth century.[4]

Troeltsch distinguished between the original gospel of Jesus and the primitive church and the later creation of a religious community. When faith in Jesus, the risen and exalted Lord, became the central point of worship in a new religious community, the necessity for organization arose. From the beginning of this organization, according to Troeltsch, three major types of sociological development can be observed:

1. the church
2. the sect
3. mysticism

To appreciate Baptists' shaping of Jesus, the distinction between the church and the sect is vital.

With the church, focus is on an institution endowed with grace and salvation as a result of the work of redemption. It is able to receive the masses and to adjust itself to the world. For the sake of the objective treasures of grace and of redemption, the church can afford to ignore the need for subjective holiness. In Troeltsch's scheme, the Christ of the church is the redeemer, who in his work of salvation has achieved redemption, once for all. Working marvelously through the ministry, the word, and the sacraments in the church, he imparts to individuals the benefits of his saving work.

The sect is a voluntary society composed of Christian believers who are bound to each other by the experience of the "new birth." These believers are separated from the world, and in varying degrees within their own group set up the Christian order, based on love. The sects emphasize the law instead of grace and live in expectation of and in preparation for the coming kingdom of God.

The Christ of the sect is the Lord, the example and lawgiver of divine authority and dignity, who allows his elect to pass through contempt and misery on their earthly pilgrimage, but who will complete the real work of redemption at his return, when he will establish the kingdom of God.

The "Christ dogma" in its various transformations is related to but different from Jesus' proclamation of the kingdom. The dogma of the divinity of Christ first arose out of the worship of Christ, and this worship developed from the necessity felt by the new spiritual community for meeting together. Just as there was development in the idea of Christ then, there was development in the doctrine of the kingdom.

The church is the kingdom of Christ, and is therefore identical with the kingdom of God in the world, or at any rate it is the method by which it is continually produced afresh. In the sect Jesus is still the herald of the kingdom of God that he ushers in himself; the sect is inclined to emphasis upon the second advent of Jesus Christ.

The doctrine of redemption undergoes a process similar to that with the kingdom of God. From the viewpoint of the church, the work of redemption was finished by the atoning death of Christ; this "finished work" endows the church with the power to transmit remission of sins and sanctification. The sect believes that real redemption lies in the advent of Christ and the establishment of the Kingdom; the whole previous process of history was a mere preparation for this consummation.

Each of the different images of Jesus possesses a relationship to the historical message of Jesus, but no one of the images expresses that message in its entirety according to Troeltsch. The churchly image of Jesus mediates the universality of Jesus, but it combines with sacrament and institution what does not conform directly with the proclamation of Jesus. The image of Jesus of the sect type realizes the unconditioned religious-ethical nature of Jesus, although it does so in a dogmatic static fashion that does not conform to its inner freedom.

The Church in Pilgrimage and the Dynamic Shaping of Jesus Christ

The Puritan-Separatist-Baptist trajectory allows us to appreciate different ways of bringing the story of Jesus to bear on the life of the world, different ways to shape Jesus. There is the sacramental perspective of the grace of Christ flowing to a waiting world and the evangelical perspective of justification by grace alone. There is also the gospel perspective of serving as agent of God in the world, doing the good that follows upon the way of Christ.

The shaping of Jesus by the way that General Baptists and Particular Baptists viewed and practiced church—vis-à-vis the Roman Catholic Church, the Church of England, and the other mainline Reformation bodies—may be illuminated by the suggestion of Klaus Haacker, a German New Testament scholar, as to how Jesus has been shaped in historical study. What Haacker says is valid for the whole course of the imaging of Jesus, including the imaging within the two natures model and the historical model. He says that "the changing and competing images of Jesus would be understood better as the result of an interaction between the historical data and the assumptions of the researchers and their time."[5] He sees three interrelated factors at work in the overall imaging of Jesus:

1. evidence
2. relevance
3. emergence

Evidence is related to the fact that the study of Jesus involves objective material data. The Gospels are the basic sources. Relevance has to do with the judgment of value for believers personally and socially. Emergence is the constructive interplay of the evidence and relevance in the process of perception. The emergence Haacker has in mind is similar to the way a picture gradually emerges when a photograph is developed. There is an objective, material element that insures the outline of the whole. But there is a variability of light and darkness insofar as the parts of the picture are concerned. "So the textual foundation for Jesus study remains stable to a large extent. But the interpretation can expose certain parts of the tradition in a stronger fashion (through frequent citations, for example) and underexpose other parts of the tradition so as to allow them to remain faint."[6]

The model for study Haacker suggests combines "scientific" and "poetic" moves, "modern" and "postmodern" moves. The data uncovered by contemporary theological, historical-critical, and literary methods are completed by frameworks for understanding that do not arise in the data themselves. Imaginative operations of the scholar remain necessary.

The fact that the study of Jesus is a poetic study and each of the different Jesuses created is satisfying as it "fits" the critical data and the cultural and theological worldview of their creator does not mean that Jesus is simply an imaginative figure. The figure of Jesus is not so subject to the background, motives, and activities of Christians that the Jesuses of historical imagination are merely self-portraits of their authors. They are not totally dependent upon the reigning theological and cultural paradigms.

There is a range of images, to be sure, as all the accounts of Jesus go beyond the sources to make sense of the sources and the data in the sources. Religious symbols, images, and stories of Jesus have been continually reinterpreted in the church. And historical hypotheses have been continually transformed and redefined. But there is a clear identification: The same sources are used, the same basic sayings of Jesus are quoted, and the same individuals and groups of persons around Jesus are found.

The Baptist emphasis upon dynamic confessional statements rather than static creedal statements fits the perspective of Haacker. In his advice to the Pilgrim fathers before they left for America, John Robinson contrasted the "free church" and other Protestants in terms of this dynamic:

> I cannot sufficiently bewail the condition of the Reformed churches, who are come to a Period in religion and will go at present no further than the instruments of their reformation. The Lutherans can't be drawn to go beyond what Luther saw; whatever part of his will God has revealed to Calvin they would rather die than embrace it; and the Calvinists you see, stick fast where they were left by that great man of God, who yet saw not all things. . . . I beseech you remember it is an article of your church covenant, that you be ready to receive whatever truth shall be made known to you from the written word of God.[7]

The following two chapters treat the resources for the shaping of Jesus provided by the New Testament and the early creeds of the church. These may be thought of as "foundational" shapings. Nevertheless, the call for interpretation of the Bible within the church and the provisional nature of the church results in a creative biblical hermeneutics that goes beyond these foundations and justifies a dynamic shaping of Jesus Christ.

Notes

[1]Champlin Burrage, *The Early English Dissenters in the Light of Recent Research* (New York: Russell and Russell, 1967), 1, 80. Cited from H. Leon McBeth, *The Baptist Heritage: Four Centuries of Baptist Witness* (Nashville, Broadman Press, 1987), 26. The discussion of Baptist beginnings in this chapter relies upon the dependable and comprehensive work of McBeth.

[2]McBeth, *The Baptist Heritage*, 32.

[3]Ibid., 34.

[4]See Ernst Troeltsch, *The Social Teaching of the Christian Churches* (London: George Allen & Unwin; New York: Macmillan, 1931), 2, 993-95.

[5]Klaus Haacker, "Die Moderne Historische Jesus-Forschung als Hermeneutisches Problem," *Theologische Beiträge* 31 (2000) 62.

[6]Ibid., 63.

[7]Daniel Neal, *History of the Puritans*, part 2, chap. 2. Quoted in Ernest Payne, *The Fellowship of Believers* (London: Cary Kingsgate Press, 1952), 74.

CHAPTER 2

Jesus as "Christ" and "Lord"

New Testament Confessions and Hymns

From the beginning of the Jesus movement, followers experienced and shaped Jesus in ways that matched their different needs and abilities. In the primitive oral and written traditions that came to fixed expression within the text of the New Testament we find Jesus shaped as "Christ" and "Lord" from the background of the Jewish hope of a new age. And in the later creeds of the church that defined orthodoxy, Jesus is shaped as "Truly God and Truly Man" from the perspective of metaphysical argumentation. Other titles from the Jewish perspective spoke of the hope of a new age: Son of God, Son of Man, prophet, wisdom.

By the time of Ignatius of Antioch (ca. 50–107 CE), however, the shaping of Jesus was already developing in the pattern to be seen in the ecumenical councils. In his letter to the Ephesians, Ignatius speaks of Jesus as "our God, Jesus (the) Christ" and states that "there is one physician, who is both flesh and spirit, born and yet not born, who is God in man, true life-and-death, both of Mary and of God, first passible then impassible, Jesus Christ our Lord."[1]

Different sorts of understandings and shapings of Jesus have been correlated in the life and liturgy of the church. Old Testament and New Testament readings have been connected Sunday by Sunday, with the readings of the Old Testament influencing the shaping of Jesus through a typological hermeneutic. Jesus is seen, for example, as the "servant" of Isaiah. The literary accounts of Jesus as teacher and performer of extraordinary deeds and early Christian hymns and confessions of Jesus as Christ and Lord have also been set into the philosophical and theological framework provided by the ancient creeds recited weekly.

In the twenty-first century we are now able to look at the New Testament resources (the ancient hymns, confessions, Christological affirmations in the letters and epistles, and teachings and narratives about Jesus in the Gospels) as shaping of Jesus that took place in creative artistic terms that did justice to the followers' experience of Jesus. And we distinguish those shapings from the shapings of the creeds governed by philosophical and theological conventions and conceptions of humanity and divinity.

When we read the New Testament writings without the benefit of historical consciousness, we are in danger of reading back into the New Testament the problem of the post-New Testament church and its formulation of Christology. A more-or-less literalistic credulous approach is tempting. The result: the creeds called Jesus "God," so the earliest disciples must have called Jesus "God" even during his ministry. In his study of the question of the New Testament witness to the divinity of Jesus, the Roman Catholic New Testament scholar Raymond E. Brown affirmed the church's confession of Jesus Christ as the God-Man, but he cautioned against a simplistic confusion of the New Testament existential and liturgical ambiance and the essentialist definitions of the creeds. This confusion affects the shaping of Jesus as the God-man.

> Many Christian believers do not sufficiently appreciate the humanity of Jesus. They transfer the picture of the glorified Jesus back into his public ministry, imagining him to have walked through Galilee with an aura and a halo about him. They cannot imagine him as being like other men; and they are embarrassed by the Gospel vignettes of Jesus as sometimes tired and dirty, annoyed and tempted, indistinguishable in a crowd, treated as a fanatic and rabble-rouser.[2]

Brown studied the New Testament passages that use "God" for Jesus and declared that the instances in the New Testament with Jesus called God are not attempts to define Jesus essentially. Even in the first chapter of the Gospel of John, the approach is largely functional, although that passage raises questions of more than a functional nature. Brown concludes:

> The acclamation of Jesus as God is a response of prayer and worship to the God who has revealed himself to men in Jesus . . . [E]ven though we have seen that there is a solid

biblical precedent for calling Jesus God, we must be cautious to evaluate this usage in terms of the New Testament ambiance. Our firm adherence to the later theological and ontological developments in the meaning of the formula "Jesus is God" must not cause us to overvalue or undervalue the New Testament confession.[3]

Brown's caution is valuable for appreciating Baptist shapings of Jesus in the past and present. The New Testament ambiance for the shaping of Jesus is not the same as that of the church councils or that of the present day.

The Primitive Literary Shaping: Early Christian Confessions

The earliest followers of Jesus Christ meditated worshipfully on the person and work of Jesus of Nazareth. In the process of expressing their faith in Jesus they developed confessions, or formulaic statements of Christian conviction. These confessions ranged from single-statement affirmations to hymns and prose confessions.[4] The Hebrew Bible and the Jewish patterns of interpreting the Bible provided the primitive Christian community resources for this meditation and therefore for understanding and shaping Jesus. The word "Lord" (Greek: *kyrios*) is used to translate "Yahweh," the covenant name for God, in the Septuagint. The word "Christ" is the Greek translation of the Hebrew word "Messiah" or "Anointed." This is the title used of the king of Israel.

The Gospels provide a suggestive episode with the specific theme of Jesus' identity (Matt. 16:13-20, Mark 8:27-33, Luke 9:18-22). Jesus asks, "Who do people say that I am?" After the disciples respond: "John the Baptist, Elijah, or one of the prophets," Jesus asks, "Who do you say that I am?" In the episode as presented by Mark, Peter blurts out what would have been a pre-Easter hope and expectation of the original disciples of Jesus: "You are the Messiah" (8:29). In Mark's account, Jesus replaces the title "Messiah" with the title "Son of Man" and cautions secrecy about messiahship. In Matthew this confession with Jesus' response develops into a pointed confession of the significance of Jesus and the church. Peter declares, "You are the Messiah, the son of the living God." Jesus responds:

> Blessed are you, Simon son of Jonah! For flesh and blood has not revealed this to you, but my Father in heaven. And I tell you, you are Peter, and on this rock I will build my church, and the gates of Hades will not prevail against it.

> I will give you the keys of the kingdom of heaven, and whatever you bind on earth will be bound in heaven, and whatever you loose on earth will be loosed in heaven. (Matt. 16:17-19)

The contrast of Son of Man and Messiah in the episode and the caution to secrecy are frequently regarded as a product of Marcan theology, but the different titles and different ways of identifying Jesus here also provide a model for a dialectical approach with different titles found useful for the shaping of Jesus. Different ways of relating the historical Jesus to God's revelation are suggested.

Single-statement confessions that ascribe to Jesus the titles "Christ," "Son of God," or "Lord" are found throughout the New Testament.[5] Early Christians evidently cast some confessions into poetic form and sang them as hymns. First Corinthians 14:26 refers to the singing of hymns in worship. And exhortations of Colossians 3:16-17 and Ephesians 5:19-20 speak of the use of psalms, hymns, and spiritual songs in the church's devotions. These early hymns praised God and extolled Jesus Christ.

Early poetic Christian confessions and hymns to Christ include Philippians 2:6-11, 1 Timothy 3:16, and 1 Peter 2:22-23. Early formulaic, but nonpoetic, confessional materials are also present in the New Testament. Two passages are particularly important: 1 Corinthians 15:3b-5 and Colossians 1:15-20 (see also Rom. 1:3-4, 3:24-26, 4:25; 1 Cor. 1:17-18, 23; 2:2; 2 Cor. 5:19; Gal. 3:13, 26-28; 4:4-5; 1 Thess. 4:14; Heb. 1:3; 5:7-9).

Present-day appreciation of the shaping of Jesus in hymns and confessions will consider the creative and affective nature of those statements. It is a question not of critical and scientific philosophical and theological creeds but of religious affirmations. In a series of publications Larry W. Hurtado (b. 1943) has dealt with the question of how Jesus came to be seen as a divine figure by the earliest Christians who yet maintained their monotheistic stance.[6]

Hurtado delineated specific cultic actions of early Jesus-devotion that distinguished the reverence of Jesus from the treatment of important "principal agent" figures in Jewish tradition (angels, royal and messianic figures, martyrs, or attributes of God such as divine wisdom). These actions include: ritual confession of Jesus in honorific terms, hymns sung in worship to Jesus or concerning Jesus, ritual use of Jesus' name in acts of worship, prophecy uttered in Jesus' name, and participation in the "Lord's supper."[7] What could have prompted such cultic devotion to Jesus? Hurtado puts the question pointedly: "[W]hat might have moved Jews in touch with their religious tradition to feel free to offer to Jesus the kind of unparalleled cultic devotion that characterized early Christian religious practice?" His answer:

> Given the evident strength of the scruple against infringing upon the uniqueness of the God of Israel by sharing the cultic reverence to God with any other figure, I judge that the only option is to think that those members of the Christian movement among whom there emerged the cultic devotion to Jesus that I have described must have felt compelled by God to reverence Jesus in ways otherwise reserved for God alone. The early Christians, however, were more concerned to proclaim Jesus' significance and to express their devotion to him than to provide explanations of how they came to the convictions that prompted them to do so. But what indications we have are that, from the earliest years of the Christian movement, individuals experienced what they took to be revelations sent by God that conveyed to them the sense that a right response and obedience to God demanded of them the cultic reverence of Jesus.[8]

Hurtado submits his explanation of what occurred in the earliest days of the church in historical terms. Within the Christian communities of the first few years—perhaps even the first weeks—individuals had encounters with what they considered as the glorified Jesus. Some experienced "visions" of the exalted Jesus in heavenly glory. Jesus was revered by transcendent beings such as angels and the "living creatures." Some individuals were inspired to announce the exaltation of Jesus to God's right hand and to summon the elect to accept God's will that Jesus be revered. According to Hurtado, "Through such revelatory experiences, Christological convictions and corresponding cultic practices were born that amounted to a unique 'mutation' in what was acceptable Jewish monotheistic devotional practices of the Greco-Roman period."[9]

Although the title of one of his books is *How on Earth Did Jesus Become a God?*, Hurtado is cautious not to claim that Jesus became a god. "Instead, he was given devotion that expressed the distinctively Christian recognition that Jesus was God's unique emissary, in whom the glory of the one God was singularly reflected and to whom God 'the Father' now demanded full reverence 'as to a god.'"[10]

The Primitive Literary Shaping: The Jesus Traditions

The Gospels (particularly Matthew, Mark, and Luke) contain literary units or "forms" that provide shapings of Jesus that were taken up and used by the evangelists in their larger literary compositions. In the early form critics the literary capacity of individual authors was not the focus. Literary critics, however, have approached the units of the tradition from both literary and sociological perspectives. A literary approach is more concerned with the literary relationships and response of readers than with the sociological and historical shaping of the narratives and teachings.

The investigation of the primitive literary shaping of Jesus benefits from the distinction between the present-day literary appropriation of the units of the tradition and the process of transmission of the traditions up to their incorporation in the Gospels. Beneficial also is the distinction between "Jesus" tradition and the primitive Christian transformation of that tradition into "Christ" tradition. In the correlation of the present-day and primitive appropriation of the traditions, the religious purposes of the texts must be considered seriously.

Wilhelm Herrmann (1846–1922) provided a model for appreciating how contemporary readers may experience the sacred in literary interaction with New Testament texts. According to Herrmann, the New Testament texts make an "impression" on us as they did on the first disciples. The term "impression" here is more than superficial impression. It refers to a forceable imprint, like the striking of a coin in the mint.[11]

The New Testament texts are the means for experiencing the "inner life" of Jesus because they express the experience of Jesus' disciples, which is the experience of the sacred. The reality experienced, the nature of the knowledge and certainty of the reality, is situated on a different level than the conventional intellectual categories. It is on the level of personal relationship. Validation is in terms of specific spiritual reactions in personal encounter with religious realities that have been impressed upon the texts. The idea that the biblical text is able to mediate the experience of the sacred in such a fashion that those experiencing the sacred have a "certainty" that transcends rational historical-critical study involves the testimony of the disciples and experience of the Christian fellowship, but it demands personal experience. It involves the construction of a portrait of Jesus—not a scientific historical-critical reconstruction—that is faithful to the experience of the sacred in Jesus.

James D. G. Dunn has carried the question of reader-response to the traditions behind the Gospels and the process of transmission of the traditions up to their crystallization in the Gospels of Matthew, Mark, and Luke. He has examined these traditions as attestations of the impact made by Jesus. The original impulse was "sayings of Jesus as heard and received, and actions of Jesus as witnessed and retained in the memory . . . and as reflected on thereafter." What we have in the traditions, then, is not just the end product of reflection. According to Dunn, "It is rather the faith-creating word/event, as itself a force shaping faith and as retained and rehearsed by the faith thus created and being created."[12] Dunn emphasizes that the original impact made by Jesus and the later impact are of a piece. We do not get behind the impact of a saying or account to a Jesus who might have been heard otherwise.

> In other words, the Jesus tradition gives immediate access . . . to the tradition which began with the initial impact of Jesus' word or deed and which continued to influence intermediate retellers of the tradition until crystallized in Mark's or Matthew's or Luke's account. In short, we must take seriously the character of the tradition as disciple-response, and the depth of the tradition as well as its final form.[13]

The "Jesus" tradition and the "Christ" tradition may be distinguished from each other from a modern perspective. Sayings of Jesus identified by form critics that reflect his identity and the faithful experience of followers include the prophetic/apocalyptic sayings, the parables, the wisdom sayings, the legal sayings, the pronouncements stories, and especially sayings that speak of Jesus' origin, sovereignty, and fate.

Günther Bornkamm (1905-1990) spoke of these latter sayings as "Christ words," with the other sayings designated "Jesus words." The narratives about Jesus were also divided by Bornkamm into "Christ stories" and "Jesus stories." Jesus stories tell of Jesus' miracles and are designed to awaken faith in him. Christ stories have the same aim to an even higher degree but are stamped from the outset by faith and express this faith often with poetic and dramatic motifs.[14]

The present-day critical and postcritical appropriation of the Jesus tradition cannot fail to distinguish between the Jesus stories and the Christ stories and the Jesus sayings and the Christ sayings. Wilhelm Herrmann's recovery of the inner life of Jesus that is active in the world as we read the New Testament narrative in the Christian community is not a simplistic historization of the poetic and dramatic offerings.[15]

A literary perspective may help us appreciate the continuity between the impact of the Jesus tradition upon the earliest disciples, the later followers, the evangelists, and contemporary readers. Such a perspective will help us avoid the embarrassment of the credulous factual approach to the poetic elements in the traditions. Herrmann sees the reality that can "overpower" us and "lift us up" as the reality of "the testimony of the disciples concerning the power and glory of Jesus. It is a fact that they did testify thus, and this ought to point us to Jesus himself."[16] Another reality stressed by Herrmann is "the inner life of Jesus, which rises up before us as a real power that is active in the world whenever we read the testimony of the disciples. In this we have Jesus himself as the ground of our salvation."[17]

The Shaping of Jesus in the New Testament Writings

The Gospels not only report sayings and deeds of Jesus that indicate he had a special relationship with the Father, but the Gospel writers also give their own estimation of the significance of Jesus in the form of reports of "good news" or "gospels."

Mark presents Jesus as Christ, the Son of God (1:1, 11). The mighty works of Jesus witness to his messiahship, but Mark's Christology of the cross (emphasized in the last half of the Gospel) guards against an overemphasis on the mighty works. According to Mark, "Son of Man" is Jesus' favorite self-designation. For Mark, Son of Man is a glorious redeemer figure who ushers in God's final salvation. Jesus is the suffering Son of Man.

Matthew's Christological themes are Son of David and Messiah but also Son of God. Jesus is the one in whom the promises and hopes of Judaism have their fulfillment. And Mark's uses of "Son of God" are repeated and extended in Matthew.

Luke's two-volume work shows Jesus as the center of history and the climax of God's purpose in Israel.

John has the most developed Christology in the New Testament. In the beginning of the first chapter Jesus is shown to be the Word become flesh, and in the conclusion of the first chapter the titles "Lamb of God," "Messiah," "Son of God," "King of Israel," and "Son of Man" are used repeatedly. Within the Gospel of John, Jesus is conscious of having preexisted and having descended from heaven.

Prior to the penning of the Gospels, Paul's writings made Christological claims. In Paul, the most prominent designation for Jesus is "Lord." Christ is worthy of human worship because of his resurrection and exaltation.

Adam is used in Paul to explain the significance of Jesus. Jesus is the new Adam. This is related to Paul's view of Jesus as Lord since it is only as risen Lord that Christ fulfills God's original intention in the creation of the first human. Paul also uses wisdom terminology to help explain the significance of Jesus. Wisdom was an important way that Judaism spoke of God in God's creation, revelation, and redemption. As wisdom, Christ is the definitive self-expression of God. In Colossians (1:15-17) and Ephesians (1:8b-10), Christ is seen as a revelation of God's mysterious purpose.

In 1 Peter, the main Christological concern is suffering: "For Christ also suffered for sins once for all, the righteous for the unrighteous, in order to bring you to God. He was put to death in the flesh, but made alive in the spirit " (1 Pet 3:18).

In the book of Revelation, the relation between God and the exalted Christ is a striking feature. The lamb whose blood enables his followers to conquer and to execute divine wrath is said to be "in the middle of the throne" (5:6, 7:17). Elsewhere it is God who is described as "he who is seated on the throne" (4:9-10). In the view of the author of Revelation, Christ is not simply exalted alongside God as a second divine power in heaven. Christ has somehow been merged with God.

Examining the presentation in Hebrews of Jesus from typological and platonic perspectives emphasizes a Jesus who rivals the Jesus of the Gospel of John. As high priest of the order of Melchizedek, Jesus has made purification for sins and is now seated at God's right hand, a high priest forever, making intercession for the saints. But the historical is not denigrated; rather, it is accented. The historical is essential in the total scheme of redemption. Jesus was a human being—tempted, subject to death. The writer emphasizes that as a priest, Jesus had to be chosen from among the people in order to sympathize with their weakness and to "deal gently with the ignorant and wayward" (5:2). Jesus showed his followers how to bear suffering, endure hostility, and disregard shame (12:1-3).

This chapter has attempted to scan the New Testament materials as a set of sources for a "foundationalist" shaping of Jesus. We are presented with confessions of the significance of Jesus that allow and even demand attention to the faith-creating experiences of the earliest Christians. The next chapter also is presented from the perspective of source for a "foundationalist" shaping of Jesus. The materials of this classical creedal source must be approached with a different sort of appreciation. But the priority Baptists give to the biblical foundation does not eliminate the need to correlate the two different sorts of foundationalist resources for shaping of Jesus.

Notes

¹*Ephesians* 7.2.

²Raymond E. Brown, *Jesus God and Man: Modern Biblical Reflections* (London-Dublin: Geoffrey Chapman, 1969), ix.

³Ibid., 38.

⁴Richard N. Longenecker has delineated the different sorts of confessions in the New Testament as they have been studied by New Testament scholars. See *New Wine into Fresh Wineskins: Contextualizing the Early Christian Confessions* (Peabody, MA: Hendrickson, 1999).

⁵Passages where the title "Christ" ("Messiah") appears in a confessional pattern include Mark 8:29b //Matt 16:16//Luke 9:20, John 7:41, and John 11:27. (See also John 20:31, Acts 9:22, Acts 7:3b, 1 John 2:22a, and 1 John 5:1a.) Passages that call Jesus "Son of God" in a confessional form include Mark 15:30, Matt 16:16, John 1:34, and John 1:49. (See also John 20:31, Acts 9:20, 1 John 4:15, and 1 John 5:5). Passages where the title "Lord" is used of Jesus in a confessional way include Rom 10:9 and 1 Cor 12:3. (See also 2 Cor. 4:5, Phil. 2:11, and Col. 2:6.)

⁶See esp. Larry W. Hurtado, *One God, One Lord: Early Christian Devotion and Ancient Jewish Monotheism*, 2nd ed. (Edinburgh: T&T Clark, 1998); *Lord Jesus Christ: Devotion to Jesus in Earliest Christianity* (Grand Rapids, MI: Eerdmanns, 2003); *How on Earth Did Jesus Become a God? Historical Questions about Earliest Devotion to Jesus* (Grand Rapids, MI: Eerdmanns, 2005).

⁷Hurtado, *One God, One Lord*, 100-14. See Hurtato, *How on Earth*, 198.

⁸*How on Earth*, 198-99.

⁹Ibid., 203.

¹⁰Ibid., 30.

¹¹Wilhelm Herrmann, *The Communion of the Christian with God: A Discussion in Agreement with the View of Luther* (London: Williams & Norgate, 1895), 102-103; see John Macquarrie, *Jesus Christ in Modern Thought* (London: SCM Press; Philadelphia: Trinity Press International, 1990), 260.

¹²James D. G. Dunn, *Jesus Remembered*, vol. 1 of *Christianity in the Making* (Grand Rapids, MI: Eerdmanns, 2003), 129-30.

¹³Ibid., 130.

¹⁴Günther Bornkamm, "Evangelien, formgeschichtlich," *Die Religion in Geschichte und Gegenwart*, 3rd ed. (Tübingen: Mohr-Siebeck, 1958) 2:749-53; "Formen und Gattungen im Neuen Testament." Ibid., 2:999-1005.

¹⁵Herrmann, *The Communion*, 66-67.

¹⁶Ibid., 67.

¹⁷Ibid.

CHAPTER 3

"Truly God" and "Truly Man"
The Church's Search for Orthodoxy

The prologue to John's Gospel announced the incarnation of the divine Word (*Logos*) and introduced centuries of debate about ways of understanding the union of humanity and divinity in the person of Jesus Christ. In this debate, ecclesiastical affirmation of the fact of unity and the confession of unity were central rather than the establishment of the logical rationale of unity. Nevertheless, the early Christological affirmations of the church fathers and ecumenical councils attempted to link Jesus to "being" itself and utilized metaphysical abstractions that had force in the church although they are difficult to appreciate today.

It is possible, then, to see in these formulations an attempt to say something about the nature of reality. They may be seen as rooting Jesus' self-giving at the very center of the Godhead. The love of neighbor says something definitive about Jesus and also something definitive about being and the meaning of existence. It has something to say about humans created in the image of God.

The shaping of Jesus was not simply an intellectual exercise or a struggle to maintain a relationship between Jesus Christ and God the Father in light of a Platonic view of God as omnipotent, omnipresent, and omniscient. The shaping of Jesus had to do with the salvific significance of Jesus Christ, salvation understood not in terms of a one-time experience of enlightenment but in terms of wholeness, a unity of divinity and humanity.

The Early Church Fathers

The importance of unity and salvation in the shaping of Jesus is seen clearly in Irenaeus of Lyon (130-ca. 200 CE). Irenaeus was forced to give attention to the question of unity by movements in Gnosticism. The Gnostics separated the Messiah from the Christian God, but Irenaeus was able to maintain the human and the divine in Jesus by means of a view of humankind with the potentiality of growing toward God. He took the story in Genesis of the creation of humans in the image and likeness of God to mean not that Adam and Eve were created perfect, but that they were created with the potentiality of growing toward God (the "image") with the goal of achieving the glory of closeness (the "likeness").

The first attempt to create humans in the image and likeness of God failed but in Christ, God succeeded. In the case of Christ, Irenaeus said that "the Word . . . having become united with the ancient substance of Adam's formation, rendered man living and perfect, receptive of the perfect Father, in order that as in the natural [Adam] we all were dead, so in the spiritual we may all be made alive."[1] The salvific significance of the humanity and divinity of Jesus is clear in Irenaeus over against the views that would deny Jesus was divine or human.

In the work of Origen of Alexandria (ca. 185-ca. 254) and Theodore of Mopsuestia in Antioch (ca. 350-ca. 428 CE) and their successors we see shapings of Jesus that each in its own way elaborates different ideas of Irenaeus. Origen's Christology began from above with the divine wisdom understood not abstractly or impersonally but as a living personal being (*hypostasis*). This wisdom is eternally generated by God. That is, God the Father never existed without generating this wisdom. Christ, then, is co-eternal with the Father. This wisdom is also called the Word as she interprets the secrets of the mind. Origen was not a docetist, for he stressed that Jesus had a human soul that had always been united with the Word. For Origen, all creatures had immortal souls; that is, they will live forever in the future as they have lived forever in the past.

The approach of Origen and the Alexandrians may be described as a "descending" Christology. Theodore and the Antiochenes were concerned that this "descending Christology" would abolish the true and complete humanity of Jesus. The Antiochenes, emphasizing the fundamental difference between the uncreated and the created nature, saw in the incarnation a divine self-emptying that operates only so far as human limitations will allow. Theodoret, Bishop of Antioch (ca. 393-ca. 457 CE), gave a rule followed by earlier and later Antiochenes: "We 'contemplate two natures' in the Lord Christ, and 'apply to each its own properties'; we ascribe the words of humiliation as to Man . . . , and as to God . . . the God-befitting words of exaltation."[2] To the Godhead belong the miracles and whatever is

God-befitting; to the Man belong the birth, growth, suffering, and death. In exegesis of Gospel texts, the question is faced whether a particular text has to do with the divine or with the human hypostasis.

The Church Councils

In the shapings of Jesus in the fourth and fifth centuries, progress was made essentially by reaction of church councils to statements seen as heterodox. The councils of Nicaea (325 CE), Constantinople (381), Ephesus (431), and Chalcedon (451) dealt with the relationship between Jesus' humanity and divinity.

The teaching of Arius (ca. 250-336 CE) was the background for the first ecumenical council (Nicaea). Arius's teaching was designed to preserve the one-ness of God and, at the same time, the uniqueness of Jesus Christ. Arius taught that the Son was a perfect creature, a kind of demigod subordinate to God the Father. In combating Arius, the council adopted a term that had been used by Origen, *homoousios* ("of one substance"), to indicate that Christ shared one common divine being with God the Father. Jesus, as Son of God, is "begotten not made" and "of the same substance as the Father."

How then could believers maintain Christ's true humanity? Apollinaris of Laodicea (ca. 310-ca. 390 CE) apparently suggested that at the incarnation, the divine Logos assumed only a body and the Logos itself took the place of the human spirit. To counter this, the First Council of Constantinople (381) affirmed that Christ had a true human soul.

But how were the teachings of Constantinople (Christ being human) and the teachings of Nicaea (Christ being divine) related? Is insight provided by the relationship of Christ to Mary? The term *theotokos* (mother of God) had been introduced to express the personal unity of divinity and humanity in Jesus from his conception and birth. Cyril, bishop of Alexandria (ca. 378-ca. 444), insisted on using the term, but Nestorius, bishop of Constantinople (ca. 386-451), refused to do so. The Council of Ephesus (431) condemned Nestorius and upheld the title *theotokos* for Mary.

The Council of Chalcedon (451) is recognized as having made the fullest articulation of the early church's understanding of the person of Christ. The council reacted against the view that Eutyches of Constantinople (ca. 378-456) seemed to hold: that Christ's divinity absorbed his humanity (the so-called monophysite heresy). The Council of Chalcedon reacted by acknowledging in Christ "two natures in one person (*prosopon*) or acting subject (*hypostasis*)." This personal unity left the divine and human natures intact and did not confuse or intermingle them with each other. Chalcedon condemned extreme Antiochene tendencies as it rejected the teachings of Nestorius, but respected the two natures of Christ. It resisted extreme Alexandrian teachings in repudiating Eutyches while accepting the teaching of Cyril of Alexandria. In time, the Chalcedonian position prevailed throughout churches in both the East and the West.

> Following . . . the holy fathers, we confess one and the same Son, our Lord Jesus Christ, and unanimously we all teach, one and the same to be complete in godhead, the same complete in manhood, truly God and truly Man, the same composed of rational soul and body, *homoousios* [same-in-being] with the Father as regards godhead, and the same *homoousios* . . . [same-in-being] with ourselves as regards manhood, in everything like us except for sin; born as regards godhead from his Father before all ages, and as regards manhood, the same at the end of days for us and for our salvation from the Virgin Mary, the Godbearer; one and the same Christ, Son, Lord, Only-begotten, acknowledged with two natures unconfusedly, immutably, indivisibly, inseparably; the difference between the natures being in no way abolished by the union but rather the character of each nature being preserved, and combining in one outward manifestation (*prosopon*) and one entity (*hypostasis*), nor dividing or distinguishing into two outward manifestations, but one and the same Son and Only-begotten, God, Word, Lord, Jesus Christ.

A Contemporary Restatement of the Question

The abstract questions dealt with in the movement to Chalcedon are almost unintelligible to modern minds. But a basic issue of Christian faith was involved. How can Christ be said to partake of divinity and humanity, to be one with God and one with his brothers and sisters. Some may hold that the whole attempt to define Christ in terms of substance, essence, nature, and the like leads nowhere. The moral teachings of Jesus and personal involvement with his life, death, and resurrection are discovered and accomplished more through study of the New Testament and participation in the life of the church than through concern with the technicalities of Christological definition. Stuart George Hall (b. 1928) acknowledges, "A serious difficulty for many modern Christians with the way the Church Fathers thought and taught is their apparent concern with metaphysical matters about the Incarnation, with little reference to the historical Jesus or the primitive gospel as we understand it."[3] The question arises whether the notion of an incarnation makes sense outside the philosophical framework of the church fathers.

The task of shaping Jesus for the twenty-first century may not be a matter of pretending that we live in the second or fourth century, but the contemporary task can appreciate the agenda at work in the formulation of the church of that era and recapitulate that agenda in modern-day conceptuality and terminology. The attempts of two Roman Catholic scholars, Benedict XVI and Raymond E. Brown, to correlate New Testament teachings with the church fathers are not unhelpful for a modern conceptualization. The present discussion anticipates the discussion in the final chapter that utilizes the work of contemporary Baptist New Testament scholars.

Benedict XVI attempts to redeem for contemporary Christians the vocabulary and thought of the church fathers in his understanding of Jesus. The church's adoption of the word *homoousia* (consubstantial) to understand the relationship between the Father and the Son is seen by Benedict not as burdening the faith with an alien philosophy but as capturing "in a stable formula exactly what had emerged as incomparably new and different in Jesus' way of speaking with the Father."[4] Benedict finds three terms used by Jesus to conceal and yet reveal the nature of his person: "Son of Man," "Son," and "I am he." When the church took the substance of these three terms and applied it to the term "Son of God," that term was freed from previous mythological and political associations. The new meaning seen by the church was anticipated by Jesus when he spoke of himself as the "Son" and as the "I am."[5] The philosophical term translated "of the same substance" serves then to safeguard the reliability of the biblical term. It tells us that when Jesus' witnesses called him "the Son," this statement was not meant in a mythological or political sense but was meant to be understood literally: "Yes, in God himself there is an eternal dialogue between Father and Son, who are both truly one and the same God in the Holy Spirit."[6]

In following Jesus Christ as Lord in the church, contemporary Christians may find themselves influenced by decisions of the ancient councils that Jesus Christ is fully God and fully man; that these distinct natures are fully united in one person. Prayer and preaching may be influenced by Christological considerations even if we are not persuaded by Benedict's arguments and choose to use modern terminology, argumentation, and historical and critical understanding of the New Testament and the early creeds.

The contribution of Raymond E. Brown to the shaping of Jesus in both functional and essentialist terms may be compared and contrasted with that of Benedict. In his attempt to vindicate the efforts of the church in its definition of Jesus Christ at Nicaea and Chalcedon, Brown correlates that definition not with Jesus' claims to deity in essentialist (ontological) terms but with the New Testament's functional (or existential) description of Jesus in terms of the kingdom of God. A major concern of Brown was the extent of Jesus' knowledge. Was he omniscient? In some areas Jesus' views seem to have been the limited views of his time. But in the matter of belief and behavior called for by the coming of the kingdom, Jesus' authority is supreme for every century because in this area "he spoke for God." According to Brown,

> No age can reject the demand that one must believe in Jesus as the unique agent for establishing God's kingship over men . . . No age can reject the harsh moral demands that Jesus made in the name of that kingdom . . . Thus, at least in the mind of this writer, a critical biblical evaluation of Jesus' knowledge takes nothing from his authority in that area which he made his own, the area of the kingdom of God.[7]

In place of Benedict's concentration on the Johannine shaping of Jesus, Brown uses the presentation by the more critically acceptable synoptic Gospels to establish that Jesus claimed to be "the unique agent in the process of establishing God's kingship over men." He proclaimed that in his teaching and through his deeds God's kingship over men was making itself felt. From the beginning of Jesus' ministry to the end he exhibited unshakeable confidence that he could authoritatively interpret the demands that God's kingdom puts on men who are subject to it.[8]

Brown sees a parallel between the Johannine and the Nicene confessions of Jesus. He sees the material in the Fourth Gospel as a rethinking of Jesus in light of late first-century theology. Although there is a core of historical material in the Fourth Gospel, this material has been rethought in light of later theology. The evangelist proves that Jesus is the son of God by letting Jesus speak as he is now in glory. "The words may often be the words of Jesus of the ministry, but they are suffused with the glory of the risen Jesus."[9] In the same way that Brown sees the Gospel of John as witness to the significance of Jesus instead of as scientific biography, he sees the Nicene confession of Jesus as "true God of true God" as witness to the belief in Jesus as the "unique agent for establishing God's kingship over men."[10]

The Jesus shaped by Brown acknowledging the limitations of Jesus' knowledge maintains the enduring value of Chalcedon *and* the results of historical study of the Gospels. The story of this Jesus can be mapped on to the life of Christians in a way superior to the story of an omniscient Jesus. A Jesus with certain knowledge can arouse our admiration, but still he is a Jesus far from us. On the other hand, a Jesus for whom the future was as much a mystery, a dread, and a hope as it is for us and yet, at the same time, a Jesus who would say, "Not my will but yours"—this is a Jesus who could effectively teach us how to live, for this is a Jesus who would have gone through life's real trials.[11]

Notes

[1] *Against Heresies* 5.1.3. See John Macquarrie, *Jesus Christ in Modern Thought* (London: SCM Press, 1990), 153-55.

[2] Cited in R. V. Sellers, "The Antiochian School: Logos-anthropos Christology," in *The Theology of Christ: Commentary: Readings in Christology*, ed. Ralph J. Tapia (New York: Bruce Publishing Co., 1971), 126.

[3] Stuart George Hall, "Nicea," *Jesus In History, Thought, and Culture: An Encyclopedia* (Santa Barbara, CA: ABC CLIO, 2003) 2:655. See Edgar V. McKnight, *Jesus Christ in History and Scripture: A Poetic and Sectarian Perspective* (Macon, GA: Mercer University Press, 1999).

[4] Joseph Ratzinger, *Jesus of Nazareth: From the Baptism to the Transfiguration* (New York and London: Doubleday, 2007), 355.

[5] Ibid.

[6] Ibid., 320.

[7] Raymond E. Brown, *Jesus: God and Man: Modern Biblical Reflections* (London-Dublin: Geoffrey Chapman, 1969), 101.

[8] Ibid., 96-97.

[9] Ibid., 92.

[10] Ibid., 101.

[11] Ibid., 105.

CHAPTER 4

Southern Baptists Defending the Faith
Crawford H. Toy, Basil Manly, Jr., and A. T. Robertson

The Crawford H. Toy affair at Southern Baptist Theological Seminary (SBTS) in the late 1870s confirmed the conventional conservative approach to the Bible among Baptists in the South after the Civil War. Instead of the progressive ideas of Toy in biblical study, the decidedly conservative ideas of Basil Manly, Jr., one of the founders of SBTS, became standard fare. And the progressive-conservative harmonistic approach to the Gospels and the life of Jesus taken by John A. Broadus at Southern was followed and advanced by A. T. Robertson in his impressive career.

The work of Robertson was seminal for seminary-trained Baptist scholars in the south. It coordinated the historical and the religious, maintaining the historical and literary origins and the inspiration and religious authority of scripture and the humanity and divinity of Jesus (the "universal and absolute truth" springing out of the historical atmosphere of "intense racial pride and hostility").

This chapter treats Robertson's appreciation of the scriptures in light of the strict conservatism of Basil Manly, Jr. The following chapter treats Robertson's approach to biblical criticism and the life of Jesus in light of the work of John A. Broadus on the life of Jesus Christ.

Crawford H. Toy and Historical Criticism of the Bible

Crawford H. Toy, professor of Old Testament at SBTS from 1869 to 1879, manifested some "progressive" ideas in "Critical Notes" on Old Testament passages in Sunday school lessons published in *The Sunday School Times* in 1878. The reaction of Southern Baptists caused him to see that his views of the Bible were considerably different from those of most members of his denomination. The debate involving Toy was not one between supernatural revelation and the rejection of supernatural revelation. The larger part of American Christianity had withstood the eighteenth-century assault by those who rejected revelation. The debate was now between individuals and groups acknowledging revelation but disagreeing as to how new learning could be coordinated with the old faith.

Robert T. Handy has classified five movements or five ways of relating new learning to Christian faith in America following the Civil War[1]:

1. evangelical liberalism
2. modernism
3. conservative evangelicalism
4. strict conservatism
5. fundamentalism

Evangelical liberals attempted a mediation between their old faith and the new learning. These Christians believed in the divinity of Christ and the religious authority of the Bible, but they sought to express this faith in the new terms suited to current concepts.

Some Americans found their inherited faith no longer relevant. They attempted to re-establish their faith on some other basis than the Bible. They sought the general revelation of God in nature and history instead of the revelation of God in Christ. These are the modernists who must not be confused with the evangelical liberals.

In many parts of America, Christians clung to the faith in which they had been brought up in spite of the storms in the northern centers. These are termed conservative evangelicals. In the face of the tendency of some liberals to move to radical positions, many conservatives began to narrow and harden the faith. They were the strict conservatives.

Another group became more aggressive, more intransigent, more certain that they had the whole truth and their opponents none. They insisted not only on the "plenary" inspiration of scripture but also on the fact that they had correctly apprehended its meaning. These are the fundamentalists.

In a statement to the board of trustees following the outcry over his liberal ideas, Toy presented his position on the matter of the Bible. He considered his position "to be not only lawful for me to teach as professor in the seminary, but one that will bring aid and firm standing-ground to many a perplexed mind, and establish the truth of God on a surer foundation."[2]

He affirmed his belief that the Bible is true. "The Scripture is the truth of God communicated by him to the human soul, appropriated by it, and then given out with free human energy as the sincere, real conviction of the soul."³ He claimed that the Old Testament was a record of the whole circle of the experiences of Israel and that the divine truth was presented in a framework of relatively unessential things. In terms of the New Testament, he affirmed that "the centre of the New Testament is Christ himself . . . and a historical error cannot affect the fact of his existence and his teaching."⁴

One of the problems that had surfaced in the "Critical Notes" was Toy's affirmation that the "servant" highlighted in the servant poems of Isaiah was referring to Israel, while the Gospel of Matthew said the servant was Christ. In his statement to the trustees, Toy said "it may be that in some cases my principles of exegesis lead me to a different interpretation of an Old Testament passage from that which I find given by some New Testament writers . . . ; but this again I look on as an incidental thing of which the true religious teaching is independent."⁵ These views were not acceptable in a teacher at SBTS in the 1870s, and Dr. Toy resigned.⁶

Basil Manly, Jr. and A. T. Robertson

The conservative biblical orientation of the earliest professors at SBTS influenced in a powerful way the understanding of the Bible and the shaping of Jesus among seminary-trained Southern Baptists. The career of A. T. Robertson, who joined the faculty in 1888 as an assistant to John A. Broadus, shows how slowly the historical-critical approaches to the Bible and to the life of Jesus influenced studies in the South. Basil Manly, Jr., the most conservative of the four original faculty members of the seminary, provided Robertson's critical framework for understanding the Bible. Manly emphasized the study of the Bible itself, which he felt was verbally inspired in such a way that it contained no errors. So confident was he that he felt the "higher criticism" of his day would prove the Bible was true in every detail. When criticism did not agree with the traditional viewpoints, then criticism was necessarily wrong.

Manly's book titled *The Bible Doctrine of Inspiration Explained and Vindicated* was published in 1888, the year Robertson joined the faculty. Manly, an 1847 graduate of Princeton Theological Seminary, had been influenced by Charles Hodge who affirmed not only that the Scriptures are infallible insofar as doctrine is concerned but also infallible as to historical and scientific fact. (James Petigru Boyce, professor of theology at Southern Seminary from 1859 to 1888, had also been powerfully influenced by Hodge.)

Manly's explication of inspiration followed the 1881 defense of inerrancy by B. B. Warfield and A. A. Hodge (in an article titled "Inspiration" in the *Princeton Review*). Manly summed up his doctrine as: "The whole Bible is truly God's word written by men." It was important for him to disagree with much that historical criticism was affirming. He believed, for example, that if the Pentateuch were not written by Moses, then the history in it would not be true and Jesus and his apostles would not be speaking truth. He claimed that the statements of the Bible outside religion are true and that it avoids any error when it deals with the many types of human life and knowledge that abound in it.[7]

Robertson's early reliance upon Manly amid the different perspectives on the authority of the Bible may be seen in Robertson's involvement in the Tenth Baptist Congress in the United States. Robertson, then a young faculty member at SBTS, spoke on May 21, 1892 on the theme of "The Relative Authority of Scripture and Reason." The day before, one of the themes had been "The Inerrancy of Scripture," with four different speakers followed by a wide-ranging debate that was essentially another series of ten-minute speeches. Robertson was the fourth and final speaker on Saturday. The intensity of the dialogue of the Tenth Baptist Congress was evident in Robertson's introduction: "I had a sort of speech in my head when I left Louisville, but so many things have been put into it since coming here that I do not know whether I have much of a speech in it now."[8]

The widespread and problematic nature of newer ideas of biblical criticism had led the Congress to devote two sessions that year to questions of the authority and inerrancy of the Bible. In the Congress, D. G. Lyon of Yale and Harvard represented a group affirming modern criticism. A decade earlier he had advanced the idea that Moses did not write the Pentateuch as it now stands, and he presented the Old Testament in an evolutionary framework. In a paper prepared for the 1892 Congress and read by the recording secretary, he affirmed the general accuracy of the history recounted in the Old Testament but acknowledged the inaccuracy of minor details. This view, however, is not important, for the Old Testament is not simply a book of facts but "a book of truth and life."[9] T. A. T. Hanna, a Philadelphia pastor, represented a group that would have nothing to do with modern critical methods and results. He claimed that he refused to examine the Bible to determine inerrancy, for "in making the truth of the Scriptures a subject of controversy in any sense, there is some danger of degrading them."[10]

In the discussion after his paper presentation at the Baptist Congress on the theme of "The Inerrancy of Scripture," Hanna declared, "I find this rift is deeper than many of you have supposed. It is deeper than I supposed . . . Yes, brethren, the rift is deep. Nor will it grow less deep."[11] Hanna was correct; the mediation parties were increasingly hard pressed to find any middle ground.

Robertson came down solidly on the side of Hanna, defending the Bible as the inerrant and (therefore) infallible Word of God—defending the inerrancy of the original autographs, that is. But that position is taken in order to defend a more fundamental proposition—a proposition that Robertson came to be able to separate from the idea of inerrancy. In his address Robertson expounded the more basic proposition. He declared that the Bible is the Word of God because here God speaks as God speaks nowhere else. God does not speak with infallible authority in the conscience of human beings, Christian experience, the church, or human reason. God speaks with divine infallible authority only in the Bible. The Bible is authoritative in such a way that it is the sole authority in the realm in which it speaks. This is true because "Scripture speaks in a realm which is above that of reason; Scripture speaks where reason could never have spoken."[12]

It is not that scripture and reason are inconsistent, however; it is merely that humans have a supernatural revelation above reason. Therefore, when the Bible speaks on a subject, it is the end of the matter for reason cannot get higher. Humans are to exercise their reason in this realm only by coming to the Word and listening. "It is the noblest exercise of the human intellect to sit at the feet of the Nazarene and learn of him what human hearts most need to know and can learn nowhere else."[13]

Robertson's use of the term "infallible" here parallels the use in the Second London [Baptist] Confession (1677). In the first section of the chapter on scripture, it is declared that "The Holy Scripture is the only sufficient, certain, and infallible rule of all saving knowledge, fath, and obedience." This characteristic is contrasted with the "light of nature, and works of creation and providence" that are not sufficient to give the knowledge of God and his will that is necessary for salvation.[14] Robertson in 1892 tied this infallibility to a narrow concept of inerrancy.

When he went to Southern Seminary, the religious authority of the Bible was seen as dependent in some way upon its factuality not only in religious matters but also in all other areas. It was in the decade before Robertson began his seminary studies that C. H. Toy had challenged that view in his attempt to use historical-critical procedures in an understanding of the biblical text. He said that he found "the geography, astronomy, and other physical science of the Sacred Writers was that of their times. It is not that of our times—it is not that which seems to us correct."[15]

Dr. Toy's resignation and the seminary's attempt to assure the school's constituents of its fidelity to the Bible set the background for Robertson's early seminary experience. Different ways of affirming fidelity were followed. In a sermon before the Southern Baptist Convention in 1883, John A. Broadus (1859-1895) took a moderate position. He declared that it was not wise to formulate a theory on the nature and method of inspiration. He simply affirmed his conviction that "the Scriptures are fully inspired and speak truth throughout." Note the cautious way he affirmed inerrancy. He asked:

> Must we not suppose, must we not take for granted, unless the contrary appear, that they (the New Testament writers) have said just what God wished them to say, that whatever they have said is really true? . . . [W]hatever these inspired writers meant to say, or whatever we learn from subsequent revelation that God meant to say through their words . . . that we hold to be true, thoroughly true, not only in substance but in statement—unless the contrary can be shown.[16]

James P. Boyce brought out a revised edition of *A Brief Catechism of Bible Doctrine* in which he affirmed that the Bible is exactly as God wished it "as much so as if he had written every word himself" and it is to be believed and obeyed "as much so as though God had spoken directly to us."[17] John R. Sampey delivered his inaugural address on "The Proper Attitude of Young Ministers Toward Issues of the Day" in which he aligned himself with the conservatives and warned that the scientific exegesis of liberal scholars sets aside the authority of Jesus as an interpreter of the Old Testament.[18]

In a rather normal fashion Robertson absorbed the conservatism of Manly. After all, Manly taught the course in biblical introduction in which critical matters were treated in Robertson's day, and it was this course that provided the critical framework for Robertson's early study, teaching, and writing. Robertson even took over the course in biblical introduction in 1892 when Manly died.

In an essay on "Biblical Criticism" in 1895, Robertson delineated three attitudes toward inspiration in his day. First, there were those who rejected the supernatural origin of the Bible and of Christianity. The Bible for them was the product of human reason and Christianity was merely one of many religions, although it might be the most valuable. A second group accepted some of the critical theories of the first group but also tried to hold on to the idea that there is a divine element in the Scriptures. Some of these mediating scholars held that only part of the Bible was inspired while the other part was human. Other mediating scholars felt that all of the Bible is inspired but much of it is unhistorical or "idealized history." Robertson felt that all of the scholars who accepted the premises and processes of the "naturalistic school" but who did not come to the conclusion that the Bible is merely human were not consistent and logical. He felt strongly that a third group that denied the naturalistic theory was following the correct pattern. "The Bible is to be taken on its par value for what it purports to be. The historical portion must be accepted as true in fact and statement, true as other reliable histories are true . . . The Bible is all inspired and is all true, as originally written."[19]

Notes

[1] Robert T. Handy, "Fundamentalism and Modernism in Perspective," *Religion in Life* 24 (Summer 1955) 385-93.

[2] C. H. Toy, "Statement to the Board of Trustees of the Southern Baptist Theological Seminary," 8. In minutes of the Board of Trustees of the Southern Baptist Theological Seminary.

[3] Ibid., 2.

[4] Ibid., 6.

[5] Ibid.

[6] Toy became a Unitarian and from 1880 until his death in 1909 he taught at Harvard University.

[7] Basil Manly, *The Bible Doctrine of Inspiration Explained and Vindicated* (New York: A. C. Armstrong and Son, 1888), 233-34, 237, 248. Robertson's major contribution to New Testament studies was in the area of New Testament Greek, and the framework for his study and teaching of New Testament Greek came from John A. Broadus (1859-1895). Broadus himself was influenced by Gessner Harrison at the University of Virginia. Harrison's work moved Broadus and then Robertson in the direction of the scientific historical study of language. This method of studying language was unknown in English universities and in dispute in German universities, but Harrison was making free use of it. He decided to turn away from the teaching of Latin and Greek usage as the teaching of mere facts and to turn to the "rational explanation" and "philosophical systematization" of these facts. He was interested in what Bopp in Germany was doing with Sanskrit and applied Bopp's materials to the teaching of the classical languages. John A. Broadus, *A Memorial of Gessner Harrison* (Charlottesville, VA: Chronicle Steam Printing House, 1874), 19-21.

[8] *Proceedings of the Baptist Congress* (New York: Baptist Congress Publishing Company, 1892), 186.

[9] Ibid., 69-77.

[10] Ibid., 62-68.

[11] Ibid., 99. See Norman H. Maring, "Baptists and Changing Views of the Bible," *Foundations: A Baptist Journal of History and Theology* 1:1 (1958): 52-75 and 1:2 (1958): 30-61 for a fuller discussion of the Baptist Congress of 1892 and for a discussion of developments among American Baptists up to 1915.

[12] *Proceedings*, 186-93.

[13] Ibid., 193.

[14] William L. Lumpkin, *Baptist Confessions of Faith* (Valley Forge, PA: Judson Press, 1959), 248.

[15] Toy, "Statement to the Board of Trustees," 3.

[16] John A. Broadus, *Three Questions as to the Bible* (Philadelphia: American Baptist Publication Society, 1883), 25-26.

[17] James P. Boyce, *A Brief Catechism of Bible Doctrine*, rev. ed. (Louisville: A. C. Caperton and Company, 1884), 5.

[18] John R. Sampey, *The Proper Attitude of Young Ministers Toward Issues of the Day* (Louisville: C. T. Dearing, 1888), 9.

[19] A. T. Robertson, "Biblical Criticism," *The Seminary Magazine* 9 (1895), 41.

CHAPTER 5

Southern Baptists Valuing Historical Criticism
John A. Broadus and A. T. Robertson

By the turn of the twentieth century, Southern Seminary leaders were beginning to see that the value of the Bible did not really depend upon insistence on a static factuality and that application of human judgment had a place in biblical studies. If human judgment doesn't meet the biblical text, Christian faith does not involve the whole person. Spokespersons were looking beyond the negative results of criticism and advocating a moderate approach. In 1901 W. O. Carver pointed out:

> Biblical criticism is not the name of a cave of robbers or a den of thieves. It stands for method and a sphere of study in the main desirable and serviceable, even essential to full truth. It has been occupied by men of various spirit, temperament, and ability. This is reason, not for deterring, but attracting competent seekers after truth, whatever their views of the methods and results of some Biblical critics.[1]

E. Y. Mullins that same year pointed out that "higher criticism" is a method that can be used by both conservative and liberal scholars: "It is certainly a fatal mistake in earnest people to deny the possibility of a method of Biblical research without peril to the faith, when the method in question seeks simply to ascertain the facts of the case."[2] Biblical authority does not preclude historical and scientific deviation from exact truth, in the opinion of Mullins. "The Bible meets all the requirements of the religious life of man as the inspired literary record of the self-revelation of God."[3]

A. T. Robertson and "Progressive" Conservative Moves

In 1895 Robertson succeeded John A. Broadus as professor of New Testament interpretation and moved from his work in biblical introduction, which he had been doing in addition to assisting Broadus with work in the New Testament. He also moved more consciously to a dynamic view of the nature of the authority of the Bible. In direct confrontation with the biblical text and released from the need to provide a rationale for a given view of inspiration and authority, Robertson moderated his position. This was doubtless in part a result of the influence of Broadus, an influence reinforced by Robertson's marriage to Ella Broadus in November of 1894.

In a 1906 essay on "Presuppositions of New Testament Criticism" in *The Bible Student and Teacher*, Robertson stressed the result of inspiration:

> I am sure that the New Testament will retain its hold on men because of the power in it, rather than because of any theory of inspiration. The theories have come after the fact. The hold will stay in spite of all the theories. God is in the New Testament books whether we can tell how or not.[4]

Robertson accepted critical results as they could be adjusted to his views of the divine authority of scripture, but those critical results enabled him to get beyond a superficial factuality-of-statement view to a deeper view of the Bible's authority and significance. Eventually he accepted the two-document view of synoptic relationships and used that theory in his commentary on Matthew. A liberal evangelical at the University of Chicago, Shailer Mathews, invited Robertson to contribute to a series he was editing titled *The Bible for Home and School*, a commentary on Matthew published in 1911. In another volume titled *The Christ of the Logia*, we see something of a conservative redaction-critical approach—or perhaps better, a composition-critical approach—to the various sources. Robertson's view of the unity of the Gospels—in spite of the documentary relationships—has been recapitulated in contemporary redaction-critical approaches to the Gospels. In a review of a work on form criticism in the 1930s (a study of the Gospel tradition arising in Germany and associated with the names of Rudolf Bultmann and Martin Dibelius), Robertson claimed that form criticism "is legitimate and helpful if pursued with patience and wisdom."[5]

The change in Robertson's attitude toward the Bible is to be seen mainly in what Robertson did not do: he refused to align himself with the fundamentalists' exclusiveness and imperialism; he ceased using Manly's arguments for inerrancy. Nevertheless, an article by Robertson on "The Bible as Authority" that appeared in *The Homiletic Review* of 1922 gives positive evidence of his moderation. Robertson affirmed that he continued to think of the authority of the Bible as being the authority of God, but he said:

> The essential problem about the Bible is not whether this detail of history has been established by research or whether this allusion in popular language to matter in nature is in harmony with modern scientific theory, which is constantly shifting its form of expression. That is quite beside the problem of the Bible. The authority relates to God's revelation of himself to men and to man's relation to God.[6]

Of course Robertson made these modifications within the Baptist fellowship, which created difficulties for some in the fellowship who were slow in accommodating their understanding of the authority of the Bible to the views of such things as documentary relationships. An official of the Baptist Sunday School Board, indeed, wrote that Robertson's acceptance of the two-source hypothesis in his commentary on Matthew would "destroy any real inspiration in the Book of Matthew."[7] Numerous sharp letters passed between that official and Robertson. Finally, Robertson assured his critic that decisions in the area of Gospel relationships are tentative and that Robertson was not omniscient. The official apparently concluded that he was not omniscient either. They agreed to work together in the Baptist fellowship but in disagreement on that point.

Robertson and Broadus's Harmonistic Approach to the Gospels

Robertson's understanding and presentation of the life and significance of Jesus Christ grew out of his assimilation of Broadus's harmonistic approach to the Gospels. A cursory glance at the Gospels could lead to the conclusion that it is a fairly easy task to write a full and accurate account of the life and teachings of Jesus. After all, there are four Gospel accounts in the New Testament. The task is simply to arrange the materials of the Gospels into a unified story, a harmony. The Christian also brings to the reading of the Gospels the concept of Jesus from his or her religious tradition. The church's proclamation of Jesus Christ as Lord and the carefully developed doctrines of the church naturally influence the concept of Jesus gained in a reading of the Gospels. The task of organizing the materials of the Gospels into one harmonious account was basically the method of the ancients. The title of one of the most important harmonies, that by the reformed theologian Andrew Osiander in the sixteenth century, describes the method used:

> *Greek and Latin Gospel Harmony in Four Books in Which the Gospel Story Is Combined According to the Four Evangelist in Such a Way that No Word of Any One of Them Is Omitted, No Foreign Word Added, the Order of None of Them is Disturbed, and Nothing Is Displaced, in Which, However, the Whole Is Marked by Letters and Signs Which Permit One to See at a First Glance the Points Peculiar to Each Evangelist, Those Which He Has in Common with the Others, and with Which of Them.*

The harmonizing of the Gospels and the interpretation of the resultant story of Jesus continued into the twentieth century in the work of Broadus and Robertson. The Broadus *Harmony* was written partly because of Robertson's suggestion to his older associate, and at the beginning Robertson used this *Harmony* in his classes. Broadus's work was a modification of the harmonies of Edward Robinson and George W. Clark that had been used previously. These older works depended upon the framework of the Gospel of John and were constructed around the various feasts in John's account of Jesus' life. Each of the harmonies discussed the events prior to the first Passover, then the first Passover and the events until the second, then the second Passover and the events until the third, then the third Passover up to the Feast of Tabernacles, then the Feast of Tabernacles until the fourth and last Passover, then the ensuing events.

Broadus felt that the "inner movements" were more important than the external matter of feasts, and he determined to construct his harmony on this new principle.

> It is quite impossible to determine with any great confidence whether the feast of John 5:1 was a passover, and the two known passovers of John 2:13 and 6:4 have really no important relation to the development of our Lord's ministry. Besides, the length of his ministry, and the

dates of his birth and death, cannot be precisely fixed. But cease to labor for an exact chronology, quit regarding the feasts (except the last Passover) as important epochs in his work, and you presently perceive that his ministry divides itself easily into well-defined periods, in each of which you can trace a gradual progress, (a) in our Lord's self-manifestation, (b) in the hostility of his enemies, and c) in his training of the Twelve Apostles. Thus we become able to follow the *inner movements* of the history, toward that long-delayed, but foreseen and inevitable collision, in which, beyond all other instances, the wrath of man was made to praise God.[8]

The Broadus work, of course, made use of the Fourth Gospel and presupposed the validity of using the materials of all four Gospels as pure historical data in reconstructing the life of Jesus.[9] Robertson included the Fourth Gospel as Broadus had done and took Broadus's lead in departing from the old plan of following the feasts as the turning points in the life of Christ. He desired to show the inner movements of the historical developments in the life of Christ as Broadus had done.[10]

Robertson's acceptance of the fact that Matthew and Luke used the Gospel of Mark in writing their Gospels was a move beyond the work of Broadus. Several of Robertson's original notes indicate this. He says concerning Mark 2:1-12 and the parallel accounts in Matthew and Luke: "Note the parenthetic explanation of the writers in the middle of the saying of Jesus. It is proof that each of the Gospels had the same written source here or rather, as we know otherwise, that Matthew and Luke had Mark before them."[11]

In section fifty-five he calls attention to a block of material in Matthew and Luke that Mark does not have and concludes, "Here we have only Matthew and Luke, a block from the Logia of Matthew."[12] Robertson's acceptance of synoptic source criticism caused him to change the arrangement of the Gospels on the page. Whereas Broadus arranged the columns into Matthew, Mark, Luke, and John from left to right, Robertson changed the order to Mark, Matthew, Luke, and John. It is interesting to note that the harmonies of Burton and Goodspeed and Kerr continued to arrange the columns as Robinson, Clark, and Broadus had done into Matthew, Mark, Luke (and John, for those who contain it) as has the modern *Gospel Parallels*.

The major contribution of Robertson in his *Harmony*, in fact, is the revision of the old Broadus *Harmony* in light of synoptic criticism. He acknowledged this in his preface: "A generation has passed by and it is meet that the work of Broadus should be reviewed in the light of modern synoptic criticism and research into every phase of the life of Christ."[13] It appears to be even more than a revision in the light of modern synoptic criticism as it approaches an attempt to vindicate the older study of the life of Christ in the face of the light that had been shed since Broadus wrote. Robertson's use of the Fourth Gospel attests to his feeling that it is historical and necessary in a presentation of the life of Christ. He realized there was much difference of opinion concerning the use of this Gospel.

> The progress in synoptic criticism emphasized the difference in subject matter and style between the Synoptic Gospels and the Fourth Gospel as appears in the works of Huck, Campbell, and Burton and Goodspeed that give only the Synoptic Gospels. . . .
>
> It is true there is a great similarity in language and style between the narrative parts of the book and the discourses of Jesus. It is affirmed that the writer has colored the speeches of Jesus with his own style or even made up the dialogues so that they are without historical value or at least on a much lower plane than the Synoptic Gospels as objective history. There is something in this point, but one must remember that the Synoptic Gospels vary in their manner of reporting the speeches of Jesus and aim to give the substance rather than the precise words of the Master in all instances . . .
>
> For myself I see too much of Christ in the Fourth Gospel in the most realistic and dramatic form to be mere invention. We can enlarge our conception of Christ to make room for the Fourth Gospel.[14]

Although he accepted the fact that Matthew and Luke used Mark, Robertson gave notes throughout his *Harmony* and at the conclusion that attempted to harmonize the differences in the various accounts.[15] He felt, just as Broadus, that the materials in the Gospels (as far as they go) can be relied on to give an objective historical account of the life and ministry of Christ.

Robertson and the Story of Jesus

Robertson's faithful mapping of the story of Jesus to the life of the believer and the figure of Jesus to the being of God is seen in *Epochs in the Life of Jesus: A Study of Development and Struggle in the Messiah's Work* (1907). This volume grew out of popular lectures given at the summer Chautauqua at Pertle Springs, Missouri, in 1906. The work is designed to be useful to those who "desire positive presentation of the career of Jesus in the light of modern knowledge and in full sympathy with the position given to Christ in the Gospels."[16]

Robertson stressed "development" and "struggle," specifically "the titanic struggle that Jesus had with ecclesiastical tyranny and bigotry."[17] "Here is the man who laid most stress on the spiritual and moral aspects of religion in the midst of teachers who tithed mint, anise, and cumin."[18] Jesus, then, was a religious hero; but he was more. It is "out of an atmosphere of intense racial pride and hostility" that "universal and absolute truth" sprang. Here is one who "made the greatest claims for himself, who put himself on a par with the living God, according to the testimony of the Gospels which bring us the story of his career."[19]

Robertson accented the "turning points" in the career of Jesus Christ so that the essential meaning of Christ may be seen in his battle for human freedom "in the most heroic of all conflicts."[20] An enthralling story of the "transcendental heroism" of Jesus is told by coordinating the Johannine story with the synoptic story. The synoptic limitation of Jesus' career to one year with one pilgrimage to Jerusalem, one cleansing of the temple, and loosely connected episodes is overcome by John's presentation of a "fairly chronological" story with the possibility of a career of three and a half years. The story begins with Jesus' baptism by John, and then continues in the Gospel of John with Jesus' activity in Jerusalem six months later (the spring of 27 CE). John tells of an initial cleansing of the temple that is central for the plot.

After a visit to Nazareth, Jesus centers his ministry in Capernaum. "The Pharisees had less influence in Galilee than in Judea, and here at least was an opportunity of sowing the seed of the Kingdom free from the dominating ecclesiastics of Jerusalem."[21] With John 5, Jesus is back in Jerusalem for a second time. Robertson admits that we do not know what feast this is or the time of year. "All things considered, we may take it as a passsover . . . If so, the ministry of Jesus has been going on a year and a half. . . . Jesus now comes no more as an unknown rabbi from Nazareth, but as a teacher and miracle worker who has stirred all Galilee. He has a great reputation already."[22]

After this journey to Jerusalem, the battle was renewed in Galilee.[23] Jesus called the twelve disciples and set forth the declaration of principles in the Sermon on the Mount.[24] In his endeavor to win a foothold for the Kingdom in Galilee, Jesus makes a second and third tour of Galilee and a second visit to Nazareth. But the campaign in Galilee fails.[25] Jesus reaches a real crisis in his ministry. Evidences multiply that his effective work in Galilee is over. More and more his hopes center in the twelve. To them he must devote himself more exclusively if they are to be qualified to carry on the work without him and to meet the crucial events now rapidly coming on. Are they now ready for the gloom of his death? It is less than a year to that awful event.[26]

Jesus spends his final days in Jerusalem. Robertson speaks of Jesus making "a series of attacks" upon Jerusalem itself,[27] with Jerusalem responding in the crucifixion of Jesus. But the last chapter is titled "The Final Triumph of Jesus." In the account of the cleansing of the temple at the beginning of Jesus' ministry, the Gospel of John prepares the way for a positive interpretation of Jesus' death and the relationship of Jesus' death and life. Asked for a sign for his action in the cleansing of the temple, Jesus declares: "Destroy this temple and in three days I will raise it up."

> The objection that it is an anti-climax for Jesus to announce his death at the start takes too narrow a view of the career of Jesus and makes his soul too small. He came to earth at all to die for sinners. He would not commit suicide. He would let events work out their course. He would not hasten his "hour," but would go bravely on to meet it. To take out from the mind of Christ this early knowledge of his death would rob him of the chief element of transcendent heroism, would make him a blind groper after the good, rather than the great constructive spirit who saw that the only hope of the race was for him to lay down his own life for it. But in doing so and before doing so he will do a man's part also. He will attack the evil conditions all about him in religion and in life. He will set up the ideal before men, both in word and deed. His death will rest upon a life worth living and that will be to men the appeal of the ages. This is a conception worthy of Christ, and it is the one given in the Gospels.[28]

Robertson's emphasis upon Jesus' "transcendent heroism" ties together Jesus' life and death, Jesus' humanity and divinity. But it also provides a mapping from the figure of Jesus to the life of his followers. The story of Jesus is told in a way to enable readers to "realize" Jesus as they understand the "human conditions and the various historic epochs in the career of Jesus." More is involved than historical research. " . . . [L]et our hearts burn within us as Jesus comes and walks with us and talks with us as we seek to explain some of the mystery of the Nazarene."[29] The church's concern with the confession of Jesus' divinity, the appreciation of Jesus' historical manifestation, and the shaping of Jesus in terms of relationship come together in Robertson's conceptualization. Robertson wants the attention of the reader to be focused on Christ as he battles for human freedom in the most heroic of all conflicts. But this battle is the circumstance for the revelation of the divine and the means for men and women to experience the reality of God's revelation. As the reader feels the "titanic struggle that Jesus had with ecclesiastical tyranny and bigotry," the reader will "find the Gospels luminous with fresh light."[30]

Notes

[1] W. O. Carver, "Wrong Ways of Meeting Destructive Criticism," *The Seminary Magazine* 14 (May, 1901), 339.

[2] E. Y. Mullins, *The Task of the Theologian of Today* (Louisville; privately printed, [n.d.]), 6-7.

[3] E. Y. Mullins, *The Christian Religion in Its Doctrinal Expression* (Philadelphia: Roger Williams Press, 1917), 151.

[4] A. T. Robertson, "Presuppositions of New Testament Criticism," *The Bible Student and Teacher* 5 (1906), 455.

[5] A. T. Robertson, "Review of *The Formation of the Gospel Tradition* by Vincent Taylor," *The Review & Expositor* 30 (October 1933), 467.

[6] A. T. Robertson, "The Bible as Authority," *The Homiletic Review* 83 (February 1922), 102.

[7] Letter from I. J. Van Ness to A. T. Robertson, May 2, 1911.

[8] John A. Broadus, *A Harmony of the Gospels*, 2nd ed. (New York: A. C. Armstrong and Son, 1894), iii.

[9] Ibid., 21.

[10] Robertson, *Harmony*, vii.

[11] Ibid., 39.

[12] Ibid., 55.

[13] Ibid., vii.

[14] Ibid., 254, 257.

[15] Some of these notes really come from Broadus's *Harmony*, but see also Robertson's own notes: "The Four Lists of the Twelve Apostles," "The Sermon on the Mount," "Did Christ Eat the Passover?" and "The Hour of the Crucifixion." Ibid., 271-87.

[16] A. T. Robertson, *Epochs in the Life of Jesus: A Study of Development and Struggle in the Messiah's Work* (New York: Charles Scribner's Sons, 1907), viii.

[17] Ibid.
[18] Ibid., 2.
[19] Ibid.
[20] Ibid., viii.
[21] Ibid., 43.
[22] Ibid., 51.
[23] Ibid., 54.
[24] Ibid., 61.
[25] Ibid., 92.
[26] Ibid., 97.
[27] Ibid., 120.
[28] Ibid., 36.
[29] Ibid., 5.

[30] Ibid., viii. Contemporary reading of Robertson's treatment of conflict between Jesus and certain religious authorities of his day must not confuse contemporary Judaism and all of Second Temple Judaism with Jesus' opponents. See the treatment of "Jesus and Judaism" in Edgar V. McKnight, *Jesus Christ Today: The Historical Shaping of Jesus for the Twenty-First Century* (Macon, GA: Mercer University Press, 2009), 138-44.

CHAPTER 6

Northern Baptists and a New Era among Baptists
William Newton Clarke

The work of three Northern (American) Baptists may be seen as seminal in critical study of the New Testament and the shaping of Jesus among college- and seminary-trained Baptists in the north: William Newton Clarke (1841-1911), Shailer Mathews (1864-1941), and Shirley Jackson Case (1872-1947).

Clarke is cited by the Baptist historian William H. Brackney as the scholar responsible for ushering in a new era in the theological faculty at Madison University (Colgate) and at the same time in the Northern Baptist Convention.[1] Clarke's story of his move from a view of the biblical text as inerrant and factually historical is told in his book *Sixty Years with the Bible*, and the story of Clark is the story repeated by scholarship in general. The work of Clarke anticipated the work of Shailer Mathews and Shirley Jackson Case, two important members of the "Chicago School," a school of thought developed at the University of Chicago in the early decades of the twentieth century and advocating the application of the social sciences to the study of religion.

The Chicago School had its origins in the work of William Rainey Harper who was invited to become president of the new University of Chicago in 1891. By 1894, Chicago was the home of creative and energetic young scholars. In that year Mathews moved to Chicago where he taught New Testament history and later was appointed chair of the Department of Christian Theology and Ethics and where he was also the first professor of historical theology. In 1908 Mathews became dean of the divinity school of the university. Next to Harper and Mathews in prominence was Shirley Jackson Case, professor of New Testament and early church history and dean of the divinity school.[2]

William Newton Clarke's "Childhood" with the Bible

William Newton Clarke and the theological seminary of Madison University (Colgate Theological Seminary) were pioneers in the sympathetic and positive introduction of progressive approaches to college and seminary students. Even before the "Chicago School" with Shailer Mathews and Shirley Jackson Case, Clarke applied the "evolutionary theory" to Christian experience and theology.

Clarke graduated from Madison University in 1861 and from its theological seminary in 1863. After serving pastorates and teaching in the Toronto Baptist College (later McMaster University), he returned to Hamilton (the home of Madison University) as pastor of the First Baptist Church. In 1890 he became professor of Christian theology at the seminary.

In *Sixty Years with the Bible*, Clarke speaks of a change that took place over the years in his use of the Bible. This change he described as "honest" and "legitimate." "It sprang out of the very necessities of my life and thought, and resulted directly from my worthiest work. It has followed sound processes, and stands as a genuine element in Christian experience. It was necessary, it was Christian, it was beneficent."[3]

Clarke wrote *Sixty Years with the Bible* when he was sixty-seven years old (1909), and his memories go back into the late 1840s. He presents his recollections in terms of decades, and the story from decade to decade is "a story of quiet development, with very little of sharp struggles and alarms."[4] Nevertheless, a contrast between conventional Baptist approaches to the Bible and to the significance of Jesus on the one hand and critical approaches to Jesus and the Bible on the other hand may be seen clearly in Clarke's recollections.

The earliest memory Clarke recounts is that of family worship, but the use of the Bible was "not a matter of the morning worship only: It was a part of the family existence."[5] His father was a minister who was "constantly in communion with the book,"[6] and "for guidance of her life and of ours," the Bible was always with his mother.[7] Clarke speaks of the "unconscious bondage" of his mother. The Bible brought her what Clarke called the "spirit of Judaism" as well as the Christian faith, and "not until old age did she come out into the liberty of the children of God."[8]

Clarke speaks of an experience at age sixteen when "my personal religious life began."[9] He asked his father what passage of the Bible he should read. His father referred him to the eighth chapter of Romans. Clarke admits that at age sixteen he found little of value in that passage. From this he learned that "not everything in the Bible is equally available as food for the soul."[10] He discovered that "all Christians gather out their personal Bibles to feed upon." These Bibles are all "smaller than the great book." To Clarke this meant his childhood with the Bible was ended. "Let it not be supposed, however, that the main work of those early days was rejection, or anything that resembled it. No: it was recognition, selection, assimilation. I was taking food, not refusing it."[11]

The Bible, Science, and Biblicism

A significant experience during Clarke's early period had to do with the relation of the Bible to science. His textbook on geology convinced him that the doctrine of an earth only six thousand years old—which he said he had earlier accepted—was "forever irreconcilable with geology and impossible of belief. Facts enough to convince me of that had already been presented, and I was convinced."[12] He found himself allowing science to tell him what to believe about the age of the earth. "In this my opening mind was opening aright. But I never supposed for a moment that science was taking the place of the Bible as the decisive witness: I supposed that it was only interpreting the Bible."[13] Clarke "altered" the Bible to suit the facts. But he declared that "happily, I did not know that I had done anything of serious importance." If he had known, Clarke acknowledged, he would have been troubled. "But I simply adopted the new meaning into my sacred book, and understood the Bible in its proper meaning to stand as a witness to the view of the facts which I had obtained."[14]

By the end of his first pastorate Clarke had come to concentrate upon the text of the Bible. "I was a firm biblicist."[15] He contrasts two teachers in this regard. One teacher concentrated upon exegesis. "In this there was a call for the investigation of every word, and for the most careful judgment as to structure, connection, and purpose . . ."[16] Another teacher, Ebenezer Dodge, long-time faculty member and president at Madison University, was more of a philosopher. "To this speculative work of the theologian I felt deep objection, because it was not biblical enough: it was not built on proof-texts or buttressed by them, as I thought it ought to be: it was too speculative, I thought, and grounded elsewhere than in the word of God."[17]

"The calamity of 1843" (the failure of the second coming of Christ in 1843 as predicted by William Miller) was still influential in the congregation Clarke served. He explained how "Father Miller" could have convinced so many that the second coming of Christ would occur in that year. Miller simply applied the common method of taking the Bible as it reads, applying the method to the predictive and apocalyptic parts of the Bible, and reading them in the light of "history ill understood" and "mathematics misapplied."[18]

> At first it seemed unaccountable, but on further consideration I became sure that I understood it. Miller's hearers were sincere Bible readers, of the ordinary literalistic kind. Without the habit of seeking light upon the page, except as light shone forth from the page itself, they were accustomed to "take the Bible as it reads," regard it all in its obvious meaning as the equal utterance of God, and consider it all applicable to themselves.[19]

At the conclusion of his first pastorate, admits Clarke, he had not yet exchanged his inherited view of the "sacred book" for another. But he was on the way.

> I was beginning to know how much it means that the Bible is a translated book . . . I was beginning to know also, in slight degree, how much it means that the Bible is a genuinely historical book, having its rise and habitat in the human world, recording vital dealings between God and men, and to be understood in the light of its historical origins, intentions, and development. No longer an unrelieved level of equal authority, it was beginning to have its hills and dales, its lights and shades, as a book of real life, the life of God in man and of man with God.[20]

A Time of Harvest and Seedtime

The period of the 1870s was " a "time of harvest" from the perspective of Clarke's earlier life but also a "seedtime" seen from the perspective of later experiences. It was a period when Clarke was moving from the idea that "the Scriptures limit me to this" to the idea that "the Scriptures open my way to this." "At first I was regarding the restraints of the Bible: afterwards I was following out its spirit."[21] The 1870s influenced Clarke in terms of the study of the life of Jesus. Although he confesses the passing away of the idea that a genuine biography of Jesus can be written, the "lives of Jesus brought us a genuine blessing":

> They were the popular and effective part of a large movement to bring him out of the region of dogmatic conceptions, partly unreal, into the realm of real life. To vivify our mental image of Jesus the modern knowledge of history, geography, and archaeology brought its treasures, and the great theme was presented by an imagination enlightened by this new knowledge, as well as by the old love and reverence . . . [T]he main point was that the study of the Saviour of the world, from being a study of doctrinal conceptions, now became study of a living person, into which all the wealth of this illuminating knowledge was poured.[22]

Another result of the 1870s was the judgment that the biblical writers were not to be looked upon as infallible guides. This determination came from his study of the biblical teachings on the millennium, with Clarke concluding that "the Bible contained the confident prediction of an early advent, and at the same time it contained an outlook upon the future that neither included an early advent nor had a place for one." Clarke observed that both doctrines could be derived from the Bible, but that neither one was the doctrine of the Bible as a whole. "In the sense of being found in the Scriptures, both were scriptural; but in the better sense of rightly representing the Scriptures, neither was scriptural."[23]

Clarke's study on the atonement was definitive for his movement from using the Bible in light of its statements to using the Bible in light of its principles. His study began in conversation with a Sunday school class about the words from 1 John: "Herein is love; not that we loved God, but that he loved us, and sent his son to be the propitiation for our sins." Clark was impressed with the fact that he did not know what the passage meant. He went home with the compulsion to discover what the atonement was. He read books on the subject without uncovering what he sought. He studied the Bible faithfully and found various views of what Christ had done. He concluded that the question cannot be decided by some authoritative statement—some external explanation. Rather, the genuine internal meaning was needed: "What is it that the good God and Father of Jesus Christ has done in him for us in our sinfulness?"[24] Clark saw clearly that the question was one in the realm of ethics. "The decisive factor is the character of God. The God whom Jesus Christ has revealed to us has acted in accordance with what he is. In this work he has acted out his real self."[25]

Clark confesses that he felt a special commission to inquire about the atonement. "To do a man's work in this great quest was my business for the time, and I could no more take my conclusion from dictation of the Bible than I could from the dictation of the church. I was constrained to go back of both."[26] In about 1878 Clarke wrote a paper, "The Saving Interposition of God," for a ministers group of which he was a member at Newton. In the paper, Clarke rejected the old substitutionary idea of atonement as too Judaic. He claimed the right that Paul and the other apostles enjoyed: to reinterpret doctrine in light of the needs of his age. "I was not asking what the Bible specifically said upon my theme, but was taking the large truths that the Bible brought me, and wielding them as my instruments in a spiritual work of inquiry."[27]

Movement to "Higher Criticism"

The 1880s brought Clarke to a new pastorate and to a position as a teacher of the New Testament. Some important items are mentioned by Clarke: his movement from the practice of reading sermons to a purely extemporaneous style, a more personal handling of the Bible (which he saw as result of his work on the atonement), his authorship of a commentary on the Gospel of Mark, and especially the wholehearted embracing of "higher criticism." He speaks of higher criticism as being "one of the most valuable of helps" in his "progress toward the restful attitude concerning the Bible" that he came to hold.[28]

In the 1890s Clarke took the place of his old teacher (Ebenezer Dodge, the one he found lacking in his youth) in systematic theology. Practical and theoretical needs dictated that Clarke prepare a textbook. Dodge had not left enough of his privately printed textbook for even a single class, and the existing textbooks were framed on a proof-text method of using the Bible that Clarke could not accept.[29] The practice of setting forth a theory of inspiration and the related use of proof-texts to support theological statements were not part of Clarke's procedure. The failure to set forth a theory of inspiration was a repudiation of the assumption that "if the Bible was to be used as a primary source for theology, that course must be justified by presenting proof that the Bible was divinely inspired."[30] Clarke says that a two-fold vision provided him his "key to the Christian theology."

> I found that the Bible set before me the historical and spiritual figure of Jesus Christ, and showed me the principle on which he taught us to live the true life of men: it showed me the Savior, and the salvation. In this two-fold vision I

had the key to the Christian theology; or, to use another simile, I had the light which it was my privilege to hold up for illumination of the field.[31]

The proof-text method Clarke disavowed held that a theologian must work into his doctrinal statement the testimony of all the texts in the Bible that bear upon the doctrine and must construct a comprehensive statement including the teaching of them all. If this task cannot be fully accomplished, still it is the ideal, to be reached as fully as possible.[32] Clarke worked under a different conception of the relation of the Bible to theology. Instead of seeing theology as the first fruit of exegesis, Clarke saw theology as the "second fruit." "Between exegesis and theology there are intermediate processes not only legitimate but necessary." Rather than being "dictated" by the Bible, a person's theology "should be inspired in him by the Bible—or more truly, inspired in him through the Bible by the spirit that inspired the Bible."[33] Clarke maintains that the utterances of scripture fall into three groups and must be brought into theology in three different ways [34]:

1. the religious utterance of the Old Testament
2. the utterances of Jesus himself
3. the interpretations of the Christian gospel made by the followers of Jesus

Clarke cautions that the utterances of Jesus are not to be used directly "as timbers for the frame of a system." They were spoken for "the revealing of God, for the enlightening of men, for the illuminating of religion, for the establishing of eternal life."[35] The interpretations made by the followers of Jesus in the New Testament are also religious rather than doctrinal in their intention. " . . . [T]he element of finality in the form of doctrine they could not possibly possess. In due time doctrine must pass through them into other forms, and through these again into other forms, and through these again into others still."[36] The utterances of Jesus and the followers of Jesus enter into theology through life, "through the medium of religion and experience."[37] Religion is the life of humans in their superhuman relations. It has to do with the affective nature; it is a function of the heart. Theology or doctrine is the unfolding and exposition of the concepts that enter into religion. Not only do we have materials that were religious rather than doctrinal in their intent, "they were made in conditions that were more or less provisional and temporary."[38]

The New Century and the Chief Danger about the Bible

In his chapter on "The New Century" Clarke contrasts the use of the Bible as "an object of study" and "a means of study," or the use of the Bible "in the light of its statements" and the use of the Bible "in the light of its principles":

> When I viewed the Bible as a body of statements, it was natural that I should use it chiefly as an object of study. I was seeking to know what the statements meant. When I came to view it as an expression of principles, the principles of divine religion, it thereby became to me a means of study: then I sought to know whither the principles led.[39]

Clarke concludes his volume on *Sixty Years with the Bible* with a statement of the basis for his confidence in the value of the Bible and a caution about "the chief danger about the Bible at present." The role of Jesus is stressed by Clarke in his estimation of the value of the Bible, and it is possible to relate Clarke's approach to the nature of the Bible directly to the dynamic shaping of Jesus. "It is certain that the Bible gives us knowledge of Jesus, and that Jesus gives us knowledge of God, and that God as Jesus reveals him as the true light of life. Our sacred book is thus our guide to Jesus, to God, and to life divine."[40] The system of Christian theology resulting from Clarke's approach "has God for its centre, the spirit of Jesus for its organizing principle, and congenial truth from within the Bible and from without for its material . . . The glory of the Bible for my purpose as theologian is that it gives me Christ whose revealing shows me God the centre of the system, that it instructs me in that spirit of Christ which is the organizing principle, and that it provides me with abundant congenial material for the building up of doctrine."[41]

This chief danger in the present has two aspects, according to Clarke. On the one hand there is the danger that the Bible will be studied merely in the spirit of criticism, without regard to its religious value. On the other hand, there is the danger that the timidity of Christian people on critical grounds will prevent them from holding its religious value in its true place. "I believe that the religious confidence in the Bible to which I have been led is a sample of that to which the Christian people are entitled, and I wish that all might have it."[42]

Clarke has been called an "evangelical liberal." William H. Brackney sees the title "evangelical" as appropriate in that Clarke used traditional terminology to express his thought that grew out of his application of the theory of evolution to the Bible and theology. But Brackney also declares that Clarke was the first true "liberal" among Baptist theologians, comparable to liberal theologians in Germany such as Wilhelm Herrmann and Albert Ritschl.[43] Traditional Baptists charged him with subjectivity and relativity. Benjamin B. Warfield charged him with "mere drifting" to an insecure final position. In terms of Clarke's shaping of Jesus, Warfield declared: "The new Bible Clarke has constructed for himself gives him a new Jesus, and his whole system of truth, brought into harmony with what he considers the new spirit of Jesus, is eccentric to the system of truth which is taught us by the real Bible which is placed in our hands by the real Jesus."[44]

Notes

[1] William H. Brackney, *A Genetic History of Baptist Thought: With Special Reference to Baptists in Britain and North America* (Macon, GA: Mercer University Press, 2004), 304.

[2] Baptist relations with the University of Chicago were not always amicable. Fundamentalist factions among Northern Baptists joined to form the Baptist Bible Union in 1922, and efforts were made to investigate and halt the modernism and apostasy in Baptist schools (notably Chicago and Crozer). In the 1940s, Baptist relations with the University of Chicago continued to deteriorate and in 1944 the Northern Baptist Convention approved changes in the charter of the university, removing the requirement that the president be a Baptist and also lessening Baptist influence on the board of trustees.

[3] William Newton Clarke, *Sixty Years with the Bible* (New York: Scribner's, 1909), 7.
[4] Ibid., 32.
[5] Ibid., 14.
[6] Ibid., 44.
[7] Ibid., 15.
[8] Ibid.
[9] Ibid., 21.
[10] Ibid., 23.
[11] Ibid., 25.
[12] Ibid., 27.
[13] Ibid., 28.
[14] Ibid., 30.
[15] Ibid., 40.
[16] Ibid., 38.
[17] Ibid., 40-41.
[18] Ibid., 66.
[19] Ibid., 65-66.
[20] Ibid., 68.
[21] Ibid., 98
[22] Ibid., 98-99.

[23] Ibid., 105.
[24] Ibid., 115.
[25] Ibid., 114.
[26] Ibid., 115-16.
[27] Ibid., 121. No copy of the paper survives, but Clarke's position can be seen in his later textbook, *An Outline of Christian Theology* (New York: Charles Scribner's Sons, 1898), 316-18.
[28] Ibid., 192.
[29] Ibid., 194.
[30] Ibid., 196-97.
[31] Ibid., 199.
[32] Ibid., 201.
[33] Ibid., 203.
[34] Ibid., 206-07.
[35] Ibid., 207.
[36] Ibid., 209.
[37] Ibid., 207.
[38] Ibid., 209.
[39] Ibid., 247.
[40] Ibid., 253.
[41] Ibid., 210-11.
[42] Ibid., 254-55.
[43] Brackney, *A Genetic History of Baptist Thought*, 305.
[44] Benjamin B. Warfield, "William Newton Clark 1910." Quoted in *Princeton Theology 1812-1921: Scripture, Science, and Theological Method from Archibald Alexander to Benjamin Warfield*, ed. Mark Noll (Grand Rapids, MI: Baker Books, 1983), 308-310.

CHAPTER 7

Northern Baptists and the Advocacy of Modernism
Shailer Mathews

Shailer Mathews (1863-1941) was a native New Englander, educated at Colby College and Newton Theological Institution. His thesis at Newton under Ernest D. Burton treated the influence of Paul's rabbinical career on his later teaching. Mathews succeeded Burton at Newton in the academic year 1888-89 and moved to Chicago in 1894. At Chicago he taught New Testament history and later was appointed chair of the Department of Christian Theology and Ethics where he was the first professor of historical theology. In 1908 he became dean of the divinity school of the University of Chicago, serving in that role until 1933.

Mathews was a lifelong Baptist and remained committed to the churches and their role in modern life. He was known for his advocacy of "modernism," which he defined as "the use of the methods of modern science to find, state and use the permanent and central values of inherited orthodoxy in meeting the needs of a modern world."[1]

Two essays, "Is Belief in the Historicity of Jesus Indispensable to Christian Faith?"[2] and "The Deity of Christ and Social Reconstruction"[3] present Mathews's correlation of the historical Jesus and historical interpretation of the significance of Jesus Christ for Mathews's own day. Mathews often stressed that "modernists" were evangelical Christians every bit as loyal to Jesus Christ as any fundamentalist.[4] But he also saw salvation from a social perspective that inferred the further maturation and development of the human personality.

The Historicity of Jesus

In his brief statement on the historicity of Jesus in *The American Journal of Theology* titled "Is Belief in the Historicity of Jesus Indispensable to Christian Faith?" Mathews comments on an article with the same title by D. C. Macintosh (1877-1948) of Yale Divinity School. Macintosh had reacted to critics who questioned the historicity of Jesus. He argued abstractly that disproof of the historicity of Jesus would not alter the essence of the Christian faith:

> So far as the content of Christianity is concerned, our religion would remain essentially the same, whatever judgment might be rendered upon questions of historical fact. It would still remain a living, working power through its ideas and ideals . . . It is not incorrect to say that the essence of Christianity is Jesus Christ, if it be recognized that it is also possible to set forth the essence of Christianity without reference to the historical Jesus.[5]

Mathews agrees with Macintosh that people are likely to be religious in accord with Christian ideals when these ideals are part of the social milieu. And even though people cease to believe in a historical Jesus, these ideals may be said to be Christian as far as they are derived from a historical Jesus. But the question at issue according to Mathews is whether Christianity without a historical Jesus remains what the word "Christianity" has meant. Is any genuine Christian faith, no matter what its relation to historical Christianity, to be called Christian? If it is, the word "Christian" ceases to have its old meaning and takes on a new one. It no longer means a group of ideals that unite it with and are, as it were, embodied in and guaranteed by the experience of a definite historical person. It comes to mean a religious philosophy that has evolved from a culture still colored by a religion that involved a belief in a real historical person by whom it was founded.[6]

Mathews declares that should critics show belief in a historical Jesus to be untenable, he would be willing to redefine Christian faith in a generic sense.

> Until then I should hold that Christian faith (in its fullest sense) will lose something of its essential character in proportion as it replaces the experiences of the genuinely historical Jesus with social values. Christianity . . . is more than a religious philosophy; it is a *religion* born of personal

loyalty and with the trust that comes from confidence that the word has taken flesh and has worked in actual life the "creed of creeds."[7]

In his essay "The Deity of Christ and Social Reconstruction," Mathews discusses the implications of the fact that the historical Jesus discloses the nature of ultimate reality and the will of God. Mathews affirms that Jesus unveils the way of individual salvation, but Jesus also reveals the will and method of God in social process. "Moderns" who confess their faith in the deity of Christ are in effect confessing their faith in the mediation by Jesus of "the divine will for the salvation of society and the consequent permanent betterment of individuals." Mathews declares that "with the church of the ages we confess him in the language which the usage of centuries has made a sacrament."

> Acknowledging the philosophical reservations we have about our formulas, . . . we must either take him thus as the revelation of the divine will in human society, or we must regard him as merely one of a long succession of human dreamers and speculators whose words have no final significance, because they like ourselves are groping among uncertainties, themselves uncertain. It is a choice between God known in human relations or impersonal forces, between hope and despair.[8]

The Shaping of Theology and Christology in the Early Christian Centuries

In the essay on the deity of Christ and social reconstruction Mathews shows how Jesus is shaped to meet the needs of "moderns" in their ordering of social relations in accordance with Jesus' life and words. Mathews begins this process with a positive evaluation of the church's ancient assessment of the significance of Jesus Christ. The doctrines of the Trinity and the two natures Christology are viewed in light of the interest of the ancient church in freeing the church from polytheism and impersonalization and embodying the "scriptural conception of the saving significance of Jesus Christ."[9]

The need that gave rise to the doctrines of the Trinity and the two natures in the one person of Christ was a religious need, one phase of the longing for divine salvation. The need was metaphysical, and the formula was metaphysical: "God had personally met and saved those who had accepted Jesus Christ as Master."[10] Mathews acknowledges the legitimate questioning of the finality of the Nicene and Chalcedonian philosophy and formulas, but he asks if a more effective expression of faith could be imagined for the fourth and fifth centuries.

In succeeding ages "the formulas have carried on the central religious value of the Christian life,"[11] but the terms of the formulas have gained a more complete content as successive ages have had new appreciation of the moral character of salvation. Mathews speaks of the formulas as "sacraments in words." In these sacraments people "have confessed their deepest faith that Jesus is the revelation of God, and that therefore in him and in his teachings God is mediated to human need . . . The faith has always been greater than the spoken belief."[12]

> In the formulas Anselm found satisfaction for the doubt that feudalism and a rising penitential system proposed to the Christian experience of God's forgiveness; on them Luther based assurance of divine immediacy and forgiveness needed by a world breaking from Roman imperialism; with their aid the leaders of the English church justified social service to a world that was beginning to be conscious of its misery.[13]

Mathews declared that Christian satisfaction in his day demanded the shaping of theology and Christology along different lines than the Hellenism of the early Christian centuries. "Christology must be social." He declared that "we think little about 'essence' and human nature in the realistic sense which was so important to the Alexandrian theologians." Nevertheless, "we are mightily concerned with society and the people who compose it." "Our elemental Christian faith is as much at stake today as in the fourth century. If we are to hold to the deity of Christ we must believe that Jesus came into society to reveal not only the way of individual salvation, but also the will and method of God in social process."[14]

Matthews suggests that the creeds of the past can be used as symbols of faith in the divine value of Jesus as revelatory in social evolution. The creeds speak to moderns as they spoke to Anselm, Luther, and the leaders of the English church. This new apprehension shapes Jesus as the revelation of the divine in human society. When we moderns say that we believe in the deity of Christ, we therefore are not simply perpetuating a term and a philosophy. We are confessing our faith that his will for human life is the divine will; that he has, therefore, revealed the true way of social adjustment, and that the duty of man is to order himself in social relations, and, so far as he finds it possible, to order social relations themselves in accordance with Jesus' life and words.[15]

Mathews contrasts a purely individualistic interpretation of the work of Christ with a social interpretation. Those who remain moored at the individualistic level "refuse to face today's need and refuse to believe Jesus Christ capable of doing God's work in social evolution." This pessimistic interpretation of the ancient faith sees that God "can only rescue individuals from a world which must be destroyed." To praise this pessimistic view as loyalty to historic Christianity "is to praise a defeated God and an impotent Christ." Mathews parallels the study of the "laws of the physical universe" and the study of "social forces." We study the thought of God when we study the laws of the physical universe. Just as truly do we study the thought and will of God in our study of social forces. In Jesus Christ we find the revelation of the moral nature of these forces.[16]

For Mathews the attitude of Jesus toward humans expresses the divine will imminent in constructive social progress. He uses Paul's appeal in Philippians to move beyond Jesus as revelation of God's life in humanity to faith in Jesus' divine value as revelatory in social evolution. Mathews stresses two aspects of the mind of Christ or the "way of social regeneration" revealed in Jesus: the might of concessive democracy and the superiority of personality over economic efficiency:

> The believer in Jesus Christ holds confidently . . . to the might of concessive democracy, the giving of justice rather than the fight to get justice. It is God's will for social progress . . . The acceptance of Jesus Christ as the revelation of God in human life carries with it also the acceptance of personality as superior to economic efficiency . . . In a world of persons progress cannot be made through impersonality. The process lying back of today's struggles has advanced in the proportion it has yielded to the personal ideals of Jesus.[17]

The evolutionary aspect of the social gospel interpretation of Jesus and the Kingdom of God is evident in Mathews's emphasis on concessive democracy and personal worth. In its inception democracy's driving power was not in the voluntary sharing of rights but in the acquisition of rights:

> But Christlike democracy heralds brotherliness rather than mere brotherhood. That means a willingness to make concessions, sacrifice outgrown privileges, reach equality through levelling up rather than leveling down human life. And this, the believer in the Christ of Calvary dares say, is the only normal method to permanent well-being . . . Democracy must be given the mind of Christ.[18]

Also in an early form of democracy, labor was a commodity. Costs were lowered by reduction of wages. The things produced were paramount, not the human folk who produced the things. But these cruel theories have been outgrown. We see that wages must be freed from unrestricted competition if people are to be treated as people. "The personal worth of men, women, and children must be the end of the production process . . . We believe in the worth of persons in proportion as we believe in the Son of Man."[19]

Mathews sketches the significance of "a God revealed in concessive democracy and the recognition of personal worth" in the "great struggle on in the world." This struggle is one "for rights in a democracy of personalities":

> Labourers demand some power of self-determination in the midst of their industrial service . . . . No student of society can have failed to observe that the difference of response on the part of employers to demands for personal justice varies in close approximation to the extent in which the real spirit of Jesus has found lodging in the social mind . . . [T]he hope of the future lies in a socialized individualism which is but another name for personalism, and a democracy that is brotherly. Social evolution thus interpreted is only another way of saying that at the name of Jesus every knee shall bow.[20]

Mathews's convictions about progress and the inevitableness of Jesus' ideals are seen throughout his discussion of "The Deity of Christ and Social Reconstruction." "[H]istory has shown that nothing social is permanent that runs counter to the ideals which he [Jesus] has set forth and embodied . . . The process lying back of today's struggles has advanced in the proportion it has yielded to the personal ideals of Jesus."[21]

Mathews's robust Christian faith is seen in the implications he draws for ecumenism and for missionary activity. He declares:

> [I]n this common faith and common hope with which the church faces a common task [the faith and hope that "the example and spirit of Jesus are the keys to unlock social difficulties"] is the centre of a veritable Christian unity. Differing as Christians have and probably will in confessions and in politics, they can find in this central belief as to the significance of Christ a focus of worship and of service.[22]

Mathews applies to economic systems of non-Christian nations his conviction that the attitude of Jesus toward humans expresses the divine will imminent in constructive social progress. He questions whether non-Christian nations have the moral capacity to make adjustments in the interest of personal values demanded by the new industrialism:

> Civilizations like those of China and Japan which with other ideals have wrought out their own economic systems, imperfect and repressive as they were, cannot be trusted to bring peace and security out from a highly developed industrialism if they have no better moral dynamic than that which the non-Christian religions develop. That is one reason, and no small one, for the Christian missionary ... The only hope for the giving of justice and the recognition of the personal value of individual lies in those who take the ideals of Jesus Christ seriously.[23]

The correlation between religious experience and doctrine in the work of Clarke is recapitulated in Mathews with the two poles of individual salvation and commitment to Jesus Christ and social change through Christian values. Indeed, the conviction of the reality and significance of personal religious experience is strengthened by conviction of social change through Christian values. For Mathews the social gospel does not eliminate but rather enhances the role of "believing in Jesus."

Notes

[1] Shailer Mathews, *The Faith of Modernism* (New York: Macmillan, 1924), 23.
[2] Shailer Mathews, *The American Journal of Theology* 15 (1911), 615-17.
[3] Shailer Mathews, *The Constructive Quarterly* 9 (1920), 39-54.
[4] William H. Brackney, *A Genetic History of Baptist Thought: With Special Reference to Baptists in Britain and North America* (Macon, GA: Mercer University Press, 2004), 352.
[5] Shailer Mathews, *American Journal of Theology*, 15 (July 1911), 367.
[6] Ibid., 615-16.
[7] Ibid., 616-17.
[8] Shailer Mathews, "*The Constructive Quarterly* 9, 43.
[9] Ibid., 40.
[10] Ibid., 41.
[11] Ibid.
[12] Ibid.
[13] Ibid.
[14] Ibid., 42-43.
[15] Ibid., 43.
[16] Ibid., 46.
[17] Ibid., 47-48.
[18] Ibid., 46-47.
[19] Ibid., 48.
[20] Ibid., 50-51.
[21] Ibid., 45, 48.
[22] Ibid., 53.
[23] Ibid., 52.

CHAPTER 8

Northern Baptists and a New Historical Appreciation of Jesus

Shirley Jackson Case

New Testament scholar Shirley Jackson Case (1872-1947) believed that Jesus enables religion to be a vital force in human history apart from dogmatic claims and proclamations. Conventional critical and historical tools provide substantive material for the construction of an appreciation of Jesus and a judgment of his value for those who cherish his memory.

In Case's estimation there is no direct line from Jesus' life and teachings to contemporary Christians and their religion. The line is indirect and the relationship analogical. Contemporary believers as ancient believers stand in relationship to Jesus and his religion, and that relationship can be discerned critically as an evolutionary perspective allows the barriers of two thousand years and a quite different world view to be overcome.

Case grew up as a Canadian Free Baptist and received undergraduate and graduate degrees from Arcadia University and Yale University. His New Testament dissertation at Yale was titled "Sources of Information for a Study of Pre-Pauline Christology." Case served as professor of New Testament and early church history and as dean of the divinity school at the University of Chicago. He wrote sixteen books and more than ninety articles.

Assumptions—Dogmatic, Religious, and Historical

In an essay on "The New Appreciation of Jesus," Case undertakes the task of "estimating the worth of the Palestinian Jesus for the religion of men (*sic*) in the twentieth century."[1] In this essay, Case refuses to establish the significance of Jesus on the basis of ancient or modern Christological dogma. It is only a thoroughly historical approach to Jesus that enables us to make religion a vital force in our own age. Three assumptions are important for Case in his work. First, traditional Christological dogma does not represent "any reality beyond the sincere efforts of Jesus' ancient admirers to phrase their estimates of him in imagery and categories conformable with their social and cultural interests."[2]

Second, the new appreciation proceeds without any obligation to obey Jesus' precepts "except in so far as they approve themselves today at the imperious tribunal of a modernly enlightened conscience."[3] Jesus' way of life "is not necessarily to be our way of life, nor are we to treat the injunctions he delivered to his contemporaries as though they were a legal code regulative for our conduct and belief."[4]

Third, the task demands "the strictest possible allegiance to discoverable historical facts."[5] Case emphasizes the role of historical research and the valuable glimpse that historical information gives about the conditions under which Jesus lived and the crucial events in his career. He especially cites these chapters in his book, *Jesus: A New Biography*[6]:

- "Jesus' Choice of a Task"
- "Jesus' Pursuit of His Task"
- "The Religion Jesus Lived"
- "The Religion Jesus Taught"

Substantive material exists "out of which we may venture to construct an appreciation of him and an estimate of his value for us who cherish his memory and, in a land far removed from that in which he lived and under very different conditions, aspire to make religion a vital force in our own age."[7]

Dogmatic and Critical Correlation

Case cites nineteenth-century dogmatic and critical influences upon the twentieth-century shaping of Jesus. The interpreters in the twentieth century as their predecessors "have assumed that historical occurrences can have a genuine religious worth only when estimated in the currency of some type of metaphysical and supernatural theory."[8] But the heritage of critical study of the Bible and the "evolutionary view" of the world and history are also inescapable. "No modern writer who deals with the significance of Jesus for people in the twentieth century, and who hopes to win a hearing for his message today, can ignore with impunity either of these interests."[9]

Can the dogmatic and critical be correlated? Case examines the liberal approach as a possibility—an approach found wanting. The "liberal" type of theology, influenced by Friedrich Schleiermacher and Albrecht Ritschl and their successors, offered a shaping of Jesus that enabled respect for historical research and an escape from the non-scientific world view that had dominated earlier times but that also provided a way of supporting older doctrinal loyalties. Two major features distinguish this liberal interpretation: (1) the personal religious experience of the individual Christian, whose evaluation of Jesus is in terms of the emotion that is awakened by the believer's contemplation of him and (2) the personal religious living of Jesus himself as it is exhibited in the Gospels.[10]

Case declares that in the liberal interpretation of Jesus, justification is found for the church's more definitive christological ideas. Most liberal interpreters think of Jesus as uniquely divine, especially in the realm of spiritual values.

> As he, during the period of his earthly life and work, revealed his ideals he also revealed God. Now he has the value of God for us, in that he makes possible for the believer the sense of the divine fatherhood and the practice of human brotherhood in the divinely approved manner. In him the love and moral perfection of God became incarnate.[11]

Titles of dignity such as "Son of God," "Savior," and "Messiah" are also thought to remain appropriate as reinterpreted by liberal theologians. The moralizing and spiritualizing interpretation of liberal theology finds a fitting place for the performance of miracles, Jesus' establishment of the church, and Jesus' death. Even the traditional doctrine of the Trinity is not beyond the pale.[12] Representatives of the liberal school "have always been able to convince themselves that the New Testament writings, or at least their more genuine and earlier portions, when correctly understood, yield one's favorite views as to Jesus' significance, and thus show his thought to have been in conformity with modern opinions."[13]

A New Non-Dogmatic Evaluation of the Meaning of Jesus

The practical convenience of this liberal method of interpreting Jesus' significance for the modern world is self-evident. It serves as a way of mediating between the old and the new, between the ancient and highly revered tradition and impulses in thinking that have become more conspicuous in recent times.[14] A new non-dogmatic way of evaluating the meaning of Jesus for religion today, however, is seen as necessary by Case not only because one cannot discover in history a firm basis for the ideas about Jesus taught in the creeds or by orthodox theology, but also because the somewhat deflated concept of normativeness advocated by liberals is not justifiable historically and scientifically.[15]

Case's new appreciation of Jesus is designed to satisfy the outstanding twentieth-century demands of critical study of the Bible and the evolutionary view of the world and history. Most importantly, however, it enables religion to be a vital force. Case advises that we proceed by measuring how Jesus in fact operated in his distinctive setting. In the process, we endeavor "to take our place by his side and expose ourselves to the impression of his personality and work, even as did his first disciples."[16]

> Let us take Jesus for better or for worse, as did his first disciples; only thus can our efforts at appreciation make vital contacts with reality. The Jesus whom we know from the pages of history is a living individual who hopes and fears, aspires and strives, experiences elation and disappointments, praises the good and blames the wicked, comforts the afflicted and threatens the proud, succeeds and fails in his designs, grows weary and is refreshed, and pursues an earthly pathway to its fatal end on Calvary. This is the specific person whose significance for our religion today we desire to ascertain; and our method of procedure will be to live with him during the brief course of his activity as intimately as present knowledge will permit. He becomes one of our acquaintances in just the measure that we succeed in making ourselves his contemporaries.[17]

As we move back and forth from Jesus' day to our own day, we become aware of different levels of interaction. Curiosity, for example, might prompt a desire to visit Jesus as he worked at his trade in Nazareth during young manhood. Knowledge of how Jesus did such things as "fashion a crooked root into a plow for some local farmer" would not be of great service today. "Had we learned to imitate his skill, we should hardly succeed in persuading farmers nowadays to give us employment in making plows and constructing barns after the ancient model."[18]

Sensitivity to other sorts of value might bring us, on the one hand, to admire Jesus' diligence and singleness of purpose, or, on the one hand, suspect that Jesus' heart was not in his work because he was dreaming of enterprises yet to be undertaken. Regardless, our acquaintance with Jesus "would have had a distinct value for us when we had retraced our steps across the oceans and the ages and had undertaken again to integrate our own living profitably and efficiently within the society of which we are an immediate part."[19]

Jesus as Prophet and Seeker of Human Souls

Case devotes more time to areas that rest on a secure historical basis. He begins with Jesus as a "prophetic preacher of righteousness," an area of Jesus' activity that can be known and evaluated with greater certainty than his activity as a carpenter. If we had accompanied Jesus on his way to the preaching of John, we might have acquired clearer insight into the significance of the struggle that impelled Jesus to leave home. We might have advised caution on the part of Jesus and even professional preparation, but we could hardly "have failed to appreciate his sincerity and devotion in espousing the ideal that had appealed to him."[20] A fresh side of Jesus is impressed upon us when we see him several weeks later in the city of Capernaum:

> The strenuous prophet of impending doom becomes the solicitous seeker of human souls. He frequents the common routes of travel where his helpful quest includes even the outcast and despised social classes. This activity he prefers to a life of seclusion for himself and his companions . . . [W]e are dull, indeed, if our contact with him does not produce in us a new urge to make religion a primary concern over the total range of life's relations.[21]

We are able to gain a measure of acquaintance with the personal and spiritual side of Jesus' religion through his private conversation and public address. Case catalogues the "open windows" that permit a glimpse into the very soul of Jesus:

> His loyalty toward God and man, the transparent imagery of his parables, the disinterested idealism of his precepts, the trustful simplicity of his prayers, the kindliness of his feeling toward the unfortunate, the joy of his life among birds and

flowers, his delicate sense of spiritual values, the flame of his zeal in condemning motives and actions that seemed to him base, his unshakable confidence in the ultimate triumph of right.[22]

The Kingdom of God and Jesus' Self-Understanding

The kingdom of God was a frequent theme of Jesus' public teaching. Case sees this in terms of apocalyptic eschatology. Jesus saw the end of the present order of existence to be near at hand. In the imminent day of judgment, God would visit the earth and condemn sinners and reward the righteous. In the meantime, Jesus urged people to live in accordance with the ideals of perfection that would prevail in the new community to be established by God.[23] Case declares that the Jewish apocalyptic imagery and absolute perfection urged by Jesus are foreign to our thought: " . . . [E]xperience has taught us that a catastrophic end of the world is not at hand and that moral and spiritual ideals when realized always reveal in the distance the possibility of further attainment that had not been and could not be previously perceived."[24] Nevertheless, we prize the injunctions of Jesus as stimuli if not as ultimate goals. "[E]very responsive spirit will surely appreciate the high value of such stimulation."[25]

What about Jesus' self-understanding? As men and women of the first century, we would have been alert "to hear Jesus say something about himself and his personal significance for the much-desired liberation of the Jewish people from bondage to the power of Rome."[26] What significance can we find when we return to the twentieth-century world?

"Only as later gentile Christian theologians redefined the kind of savior needed in their situation, and then crowned the Palestinian Jesus with the new definition, could they still call him the Messiah." Jesus was not greatly concerned for appraisal by his companions in terms of dignities and titles, but it is also true that "when we walk by his side in Palestine we are deeply impressed by the high quality of his character and personality." We now seek to penetrate behind the adornment of titles to the influence of the historical individual upon our own living as we walk by his side in the ancient world. "In this intimate relationship we readily understand the disciples' desire to find suitable phrases for expressing their appreciation of the help derived from personal contact with Jesus. But their phrases no longer meet our needs."[27]

Special Acts of Jesus, Fellowship, and Sacrifice

In terms of the special acts of Jesus (so-called miracles and the institution of officials and rituals for the church), Case advocates that evaluation be based upon the personal religion and character of the Palestinian Jesus. He acknowledges that some of these items reported in the Gospels cannot be given adequate historical substantiation. "But in any event it is the quality of life displayed by Jesus in action that furnishes the basal ground for modern appreciation."[28] In terms of miracles in particular, "we find inspiration, not in claiming power for him or for ourselves to effect the miraculous healing of disease, but in sharing his love for the afflicted."[29] In terms of the institutional side, Case finds it impossible to establish Jesus' authorization of the dogma, ritual, and organization found useful by Christian groups. "These customs stand justified in their own right rather than by the authority of Jesus."[30]

Case cites another sort of significance that is "perhaps more important": fellowship.[31] He also mentions appreciation for Jesus' baptism by John, Jesus' stress on mutual helpfulness within the brotherhood of the disciples, and the strength of the undercurrent of fellowship at the last supper. "All of this has its value in the life of modern men, even though they participate in a very different type of ceremony and take their place for service in a very differently organized institution."[32]

Even without appeal to ecclesiastical dogma about atonement, the significance of Jesus' tragic death is impressive. And the world still needs people who emulate Jesus' example. "The sacrifice made by Jesus does not stand isolated in its redemptive meaning, but continues to be efficacious only when repeated by his followers in new forms of religious activities under new conditions in modern life."[33]

The Personal Religious Living of Jesus

The new appreciation of Jesus that Case encourages is concerned with the personal religious living of Jesus that is recoverable from history. It is not an attempt to seek a metaphysical justification for making Jesus the object of worship. "Instead of seeking in him a revelation of externally valid moral and spiritual norms to be everywhere and always obeyed, we tread with him the pathway of struggle toward the realization of worthy religious attainments in the immediate contacts of life."[34]

Case seeks a foundation and methodology that allow him and the Christians of his day to find religious meaning in the life of Jesus. He refuses to superimpose a conventional dogmatic framework because such a framework cannot be supported with the historical means available. The moral and ethical teachings that remain valid are those that can be derived in an indirect way from Jesus' life and not those that can be traced out by careful exegesis of the texts containing the teachings of Jesus. We end up with Jesus and his life and teachings not as static goals but as a stimulus for the quest of cherishing and magnifying in real life those elemental virtues and constructive religious tasks of the twentieth century. Case declares that a rich heritage awaits such a quest:

> We have placed ourselves under the influence of a person whose ideals, efforts, and attainments now become available for us in the constructive religious tasks of the twentieth century . . . [I]f we have profited as we may from our association with him, the experiences thus acquired cannot fail to increase immensely our equipment for efficient religious activities today. Henceforth we are without excuse if we are lacking in spiritual sensitivity, if we underrate the importance of cherishing noble ideals, if we neglect to revere the sanctity of a pure conscience, if we are half-hearted in our response to the call of duty, if we are narrow in our sympathies and unsocial in our attitudes, if we are tardy or hesitant in our loyalty to the cause of righteousness, or if ever we yield to the seductive impulse to court mediocrity in moral and spiritual affairs. The degree to which we cherish and magnify in real life these elemental virtues is the true measure of our appreciation of Jesus.[35]

Notes

[1] Shirley Jackson Case, "The New Appreciation of Jesus," in *Jesus Through the Centuries* (Chicago: The University of Chicago Press, 1932), 351.
[2] Ibid., 350.
[3] Ibid., 350-51.
[4] Ibid., 351-52.
[5] Ibid., 351.
[6] Shirley Jackson Case, *Jesus: A New Biography* (Chicago: University of Chicago Press, 1927).
[7] Case, *Jesus Through the Centuries*, 359.
[8] Case, "Modern Varieties of Belief in Jesus," in *Jesus Through the Centuries*, 314.

[9] Ibid.
[10] Ibid., 331.
[11] Ibid., 333.
[12] Ibid., 333-39.
[13] Ibid., 349.
[14] Ibid., 339.
[15] Ibid., 350.
[16] Ibid., 359.
[17] Ibid., 357-58.
[18] Ibid., 360.
[19] Ibid.
[20] Ibid., 361.
[21] Ibid., 362-63.
[22] Ibid., 363.
[23] Ibid., 364-65.
[24] Ibid., 365.
[25] Ibid.
[26] Ibid., 367.
[27] Ibid., 370-71.
[28] Ibid., 371.
[29] Ibid.
[30] Ibid., 372.
[31] Ibid.
[32] Ibid., 373.
[33] Ibid., 374.
[34] Ibid., 375.
[35] Ibid., 375-76.

CHAPTER 9

How Much of a Man Was Jesus Christ?
A Christological Controversy in England

Significant participants in an argument over the shaping of Jesus in Baptist churches in England in the early 1970s include Michael Taylor and George R. Beasley-Murray. Taylor served as principal of Northern Baptist College from 1969 to 1985, and Beasley-Murray was principal of Spurgeon's College from 1958 to 1973.

The argument centered on an address Taylor gave at the annual meeting of the Baptist Union in 1971 on the topic, "The Incarnate Presence: How Much of a Man Was Jesus Christ?" Concerned with the mapping of the story of Jesus to situations in the world today, Taylor presented this thesis: "The God incarnate and present in Jesus is the God incarnate and present in our world."[1] He affirmed that "in the man Jesus we encounter God . . . But it will not quite do to say categorically: Jesus is God."[2]

Beasley-Murray, on the other hand, was concerned to defend what he considered the New Testament teaching that "God *was* in fact uniquely present in Jesus . . . A Christ who is man but not God entails a different religion from that of the New Testament."[3]

Michael Taylor: The Story of Jesus and the Life of His Followers

Following Taylor's appointment as principal of Northern Baptist College in 1969, Henton Davies, principal of Regents Park College and the president of the Baptist Union, invited Taylor to speak to the union on "The Incarnate Presence: How Much of a Man Was Jesus Christ?"[4] Taylor's address may be seen as a reflection of the transformation of christological thought from the question of learning certain facts about Jesus and his historical setting to the question of how to understand and appropriate Jesus. Gareth Jones speaks of this as "modernity" in Christology:

> Modernity has brought responsibility and insight to Christology and theology, and a realization that Jesus' role—to be savior—is greater than any constraint upon the theories that allow one to prefer one image over another . . . Reading through the significant developments since Luther's sermons in Wittenberg, one recognizes that the really important question centers on what efforts one can make to facilitate the work of the Risen Lord. Without that realization, modern Christology and theology can be seen to be simply a long series of responses to developments in philosophy and social thought, rather than the decisive contribution in the modern effort to relate God's Word to the world.[5]

In his address Taylor began with a summary of the story of Jesus and declared that the task of the address that evening was the task attempted over the years: to put the significance of the story of Jesus into words. He suggested two approaches to the question of Christology. The first is an external approach of writing down what we believe about Jesus. The second is to "tell" the story of Jesus "inside all the situations of life."

> . . . [A]s this world and the story are allowed to confront one another, the result will be not a formal statement of faith but increasing insight—a revelation of significance—that will lead to words of hope and judgment, of gift and demand as this part of life is transformed and transfigured by the light and glory of the Christ and is seen to be full of his gracious influences.[6]

Taylor is confident that it is possible to answer the questions about Jesus in terms of our world today and the questions about our world today in terms of Jesus! He cites two reasons for confidence in the success of this venture. First, we are talking about the same humanity. Jesus is fully and unambiguously a man. Second, the same God who was present in Jesus "is present and active still. He is doing different things. What he did in Jesus was unique, but he behaves in the same way, always in character: he is about the same business and working for the same ends."[7]

The major part of Taylor's address is dedicated to the presentation and exposition of his "modern replacement" of the section of the Nicene creed defining Jesus Christ:

> The story of Jesus makes such an overwhelming impression that I am not content to say he was an extraordinary man. I believe that in the man Jesus we encounter God. I believe that God was active in Jesus, but it will not quite do to say categorically: Jesus is God. Jesus is unique, but his uniqueness does not make him different in kind from us. He is the same sort of animal. He is fully and unambiguously a man. The difference between him and ourselves is not in the manner of God's presence in Jesus. The difference is what God did in and through this man and the degree to which this man responded and co-operated with God.[8]

Taylor made four extended statements concerning the modern affirmation of faith.[9] Two statements emphasize the way Jesus is like us:

- Jesus is a man like us (and there are no half measures).
- God is present in Jesus in the same way that he is present everywhere and all the time.

Two statements then emphasize the uniqueness of Jesus:

- In Jesus I discover a unique example of what human life becomes when lived in cooperation with God. It is different in degree but not in kind from all other human lives.
- In Jesus, God acted in a unique and decisive way for our salvation.

Taylor admits that he is not as "keen" to express his own faith as he has been. This reluctance has to do with what he sees as the lack of modern-day relevance. Intellectual investigation does not end with the mapping of the story of Jesus to the world today:

> I'm not happy about confessions of faith and statements of belief if it's implied we must all agree with them . . . I'm not happy about stating our beliefs in this way if we mistake them for adequate expressions of the truth. I am not committed to a confession of faith, I am committed to a person . . . The truth about him is carried by a story . . . I'm not happy about confessions of faith if they lead us to being over-preoccupied with arguments between ourselves . . . Finally, I'm unhappy about stating the significance of Jesus in the form of a confession of faith because at the end of the day I fear that a number of people are going to say "So what."[10]

In a publication following his address, Taylor dealt in detail with questions about the incarnation, suggesting that Christology faces the need to make some adjustments in its rather literal confession of incarnation. The adjustments in the doctrine of the incarnation are similar to adjustments that have had to be made in other areas: " . . . [A] growing understanding of how life has evolved and developed on this planet made nonsense of Genesis 1 and 2 as factual accounts of how the world began. A growing appreciation of how the books of the Bible came to be written made nonsense of theories of direct verbal inspiration."[11]

The historical origins of the doctrine of the incarnation are important for Taylor as they alter the picture of the doctrine for us. Historians have shown the doctrine of the incarnation to be the product of a great many ingredients,[12] for example:

- experiences people enjoyed as a result of encountering Jesus that they wanted to put in words
- Jewish, Greek, and Roman ideas that were around at the time and provided the vocabulary to use
- individuals involved who thought and spoke in different ways and particular pressures or circumstances that pushed their thinking in one direction rather than another.

Taylor suggested that a doctrine such as incarnation "is not the unconditional last word but a highly conditioned one; not what God said but what certain people thought at the time." Taylor concluded that there is no compelling reason why we should think as the ancients thought, and he suggested four different responses that are possible in the new situation[13]:

1. We can continue to say what has been said in the past.
2. We can say something different from what has been said.
3. We can allow variety in statements about the incarnation.
4. We can say very little.

We can go on telling a story about God becoming a man in Jesus, but we do not take the story too literally, just as we tell a story about God creating a world during the inside of a working week without believing that we are actually giving a blow-by-blow description of seven days in the life of a creator. We know the difference between poetry and prose. "These stories are poetry . . . God did not literally become a man in a way that bears description (but defies explanation), but the events concerning the man Jesus did have a quality which could be described as Godlike."[14]

Another alternative is "to say something different." The restatement Taylor suggested is basically the position he took in his 1971 address to the Baptist Union.

> [T]he godlike quality about Jesus did not arise from the fact . . . that he was God anymore than we are God. It arose from the fact that God acted in Jesus in such a way that all that happened round and through him became the saving events they did. Jesus is different from us not because he is the only God-man but because God did something different in Jesus from what he does in us. God was at work in Christ but God was not Christ.[15]

The third possibility Taylor suggested is that Christians allow different perspectives, that Christians become less exercised over the literal understanding and explanation of what sort of person Jesus was. The treatment of the doctrine of salvation is the model for tolerance of variety. Different accounts of salvation have been allowed to exist in the church from the beginning. If variety is allowed in the doctrine of salvation, perhaps it can safely be allowed in the doctrine of incarnation.[16]

The fourth and final suggestion is "to say very little." "Is it not sufficient merely to recognize, at this distance at least, that Jesus and the events concerning him were the occasion, for reasons that can never now be very clear to us, which sparked off an enormously significant venture of the human spirit into the mystery and reality of God? Who Jesus was (God or man or both) matters less than what he was like and what, because of him, has happened since."[17]

What is really important for Taylor is something that remains valid even with disbelief in a literal account of incarnation. Taking the position that God did not literally become a man does not prevent us from believing that "God is deeply involved in our suffering and suffers with us" and that "the suffering of Jesus [is of] such a quality as to awaken in us or strengthen us in that conviction."[18] By modifying or abandoning belief in a literal incarnation, we may see beyond the limited idea that Jesus entered into only a tiny part of human suffering and we are able to say that God "suffers all the time: not when one man suffered but as each man suffers."[19]

George R. Beasley-Murray:
Ultimate Values in the Language of the Gospels

George Beasley-Murray's response to the address of Taylor is not an off-the-cuff statement. It reflects deeply-felt theological convictions going back to Beasley-Murray's graduate study and before. The intensity of his response also reflects the power of the position Taylor enunciated. Important historical and theological considerations are involved. Beaslely-Murray acknowledged that the New Testament presents us not with a finished product but with diverse elements with which to construct a Christology.[20] He sees it as a historical fact, however, that the fathers who shaped the creeds accepted the ideas about God and Christ in the New Testament (not just the language) and tried to work them out with the aid of concepts of the day. The conventional Christology of the church, then, is built both upon the New Testament and the fathers. Beasley-Murray judges that Taylor's presentation builds neither on the New Testament nor the fathers.

Central for Beasley-Murray is the theological declaration of the Gospel of John that the Spirit of God (the Paraclete) will reveal the significance of Jesus. "The great issue is whether in its pages [the New Testament] there is a reality corresponding to the declarations about the Paraclete in the Fourth Gospel (John 14-16). Have we or have we not testimony to Christ from the Spirit of Truth which conveys an understanding of who he really was and who he is?"[21]

George Beasley-Murray was primarily a New Testament scholar, and his New Testament studies had direct implications for his shaping of Jesus Christ and his reaction to Taylor's christological affirmation. In his doctoral dissertation at the University of London, "The Eschatological Discourse of

Mark 13: Its Origin and Significance," Beasley-Murray indicated his exalted view of scripture and of Jesus Christ. He reacted to the "Little Apocalypse Theory" of Timothy Colani who in 1864 suggested that Mark 13:5-31 presents not the eschatology of Jesus but the eschatology of Jewish Christians composed in the 60s. Beasley-Murray attempted to demonstrate that "the teaching of the eschatological discourse approximates so closely to the otherwise attested teaching of our Lord as to preclude the necessity of postulating an extraneous origin for it."[22]

The beginning point for Beasley-Murray, then, in his response to the theory of Colani and to the exposition of Taylor is a conservative view of the infallibility of Jesus' teaching and the infallibility of the Scriptures containing his teaching. The explanation of the apparent inconsistency between the suddenness of the end expounded by Jesus and the description of signs that will precede the end is important, then, because of the Christological implications. It could be argued that if Jesus was wrong in his proclamation of an imminent end, Jesus is discredited.

> Christian believers shrink from admitting that their Lord was mistaken in a major item of his preaching and not unnaturally cast about to see if there is any other explanation of the Gospel material. It will have become clear to the reader that the present writer inclines to conservative views; he freely admits that on this matter he hesitated long before capitulating before the facts. Yet facts they appear to be and the Christian must come to terms with them: to resist what appears to be truth is to deny the Lord in whose interest it is done.[23]

The truth for Beasley-Murray is that Jesus actually believed in a speedy coming of the end—which did not occur. But this belief resulted from something more basic: Jesus' unique consciousness of the coming fulfillment of the kingdom. That conviction influenced the belief in the imminence of the victory. It is more than the prophetic feeling of certainty. It is a matter of the unique consciousness of Jesus. ". . . We believe we have a right to . . . say that his conviction of the nearness of the victory was due to the clarity of that vision in his soul."[24] Beasley-Murray quotes B. H. Streeter, a prominent English New Testament scholar:

The summits of certain mountains are seen only at rare moments when, their cloud cap rolled away, they stand out stark and clear . . . Thus for a whole generation the cloud of lesser interests was rolled away, and ultimate values and eternal issues stood out before them stark and clear as never before or since in the history of our race . . . [I]t has been well for humanity that during one great epoch the belief that the end of all was near turned the thoughts of the highest minds away from practical and local interests . . .[25]

The rhetorical vigor of Beasley-Murray's response indicates the intensity of the controversy among Baptists in England. Beasley-Murray sees the gospel at stake. He even says that to follow the argument of Taylor is to pay the price of Christ! He states his view of the issue:

[A]n interpretation of Christ has been set forth among us which maintains that the belief that Jesus is truly God and truly man is a contradiction. Jesus, it is said, was a man in whom God was present just as He is in the rest of us. The uniqueness of Jesus lay in the completeness of his response to God and in the way God worked through him.[26]

It was not only Taylor's position but also Beasley-Murray's estimation of the reaction of the Council of the Baptist Union that caused Beasley-Murray's heated response. Even though the council reaffirmed its own faith in the deity of Christ, most members assumed that Taylor's exposition was compatible with its faith. Others were more forthcoming, responding to the new approach as a breath of fresh air. The "Baptist Renewal Group" asked for more such addresses at assemblies of the Baptist Union. Beasley-Murray's reaction, then, is strategic in the life of Baptists in England. Support needed to be provided those who adhered to a more conservative interpretation.

The criticism of Beasley-Murray is in fact a presentation of a rather literal conceptualization of the incarnation. The basic argument is that the new view is not consistent with the New Testament and with essential Christian teachings. The new view (following the estimation of Beasley-Murray) challenges the teaching reflected in Hebrews 1:1 that God has spoken to us "by the son" and is to be differentiated from all other men by virtue of his being the Son of God. The new view also challenges the interpretation of Christ as the pre-existing son of God made flesh for our redemption (in such writings as the Gospel and letters of John, the writings of Paul, the letter to the Hebrews, and the book of Revelation).

Beasley-Murray cites a whole range of biblical teachings that require a change if Taylor's interpretation is to be followed:

- The New Testament's ascription of the attributes of God to the Son of God must be dropped (Jesus as the alpha and omega, for example).
- The doctrine of the Trinity becomes impossible to accept.
- The doctrine of salvation is weakened.
- The once-for-all note of the New Testament is weakened.
- The idea of the coming of Christ in the glory of God to complete God's purpose for creation, judge the world, and reveal a new creation is inconceivable.
- Traditional Christian worship (prayer through Jesus Christ and hymns honoring Christ) is problematic.
- The church cannot be viewed as the body of Christ, the bride of Christ, and the temple of the Holy Spirit.
- There is not sufficient teaching for retaining baptism and the Lord's supper.

Beasley-Murray's conclusion calls for a resolute rejection of Taylor's interpretation: "What then should we do at this juncture? The answer is plain; we must recognize that this interpretation we have considered is not one we can embrace, and preach that gospel of Christ to which we are committed. But in view of the confusion that exists, we must declare where we stand. If we fail to do so, we call into question our existence as a Christian denomination today. And there may be no tomorrow."[27]

The Christological controversy of the early 1970s in England provides different perspectives on doing church, different ways of mapping the story of Jesus to the life of his followers and to revelation of the divine. The intensity of the presentations of Michael Taylor and George R. Beasley-Murray and the different responses to the question of "how much of a man was Jesus Christ?" encourage us to appreciate and recapitulate the dynamism of concepts of the New Testament and the early church.

What does the language of the Gospels allow? What do the arguments of the church fathers allow? What does the movement from a "modern" world to a "postmodern" world allow?

Both Taylor and Beasley-Murray see realities beyond a historically shaped doctrine of incarnation. Beasley-Murray sees ultimate values and eternal issues involved in the language of the Gospels and the church fathers, and Taylor sees a revelation of the divine in the mapping of the story of Jesus to the life of his followers.

Notes

[1] Michael Taylor, "The Incarnate Presence: How Much of a Man Was Jesus Christ?" (Paper presented at the annual meeting of the Baptist Union, 1971), 12.

[2] Ibid., 2.

[3] George R. Beasley-Murray, "The Christological Controversy in the Baptist Union" (Privately published), 2, 6.

[4] Henton Davies later declared that Michael Taylor's address provided "something radically different from what I anticipated." Paul Beasley-Murray, *Fearless for Truth: A Personal Portrait of the Life of George Beasley-Murray* (Carlisle, Cumbria: Paternoster Press, 2002), 148, n. 77.

[5] Gareth Jones, "Modern Christology," *Jesus in History, Thought, and Culture: An Encyclopedia*, ed. Leslie Houldon, vol. 1 (Santa Barbara: ABC-Clio, 2003), 179.

[6] Taylor, "Incarnate Presence" 11.

[7] Ibid., 12.

[8] Ibid., 2.

[9] Ibid., 2-6.

[10] Ibid., 7-10.

[11] Michael Taylor, *A Plain Man's Guide to the Incarnation* (Loughborough, Leics: ONE Publications, 1977), 3.

[12] Ibid., 6.

[13] Ibid., 7.

[14] Ibid., 8.

[15] Ibid.

[16] Ibid.

[17] Ibid., 8-9.

[18] Ibid., 10.

[19] Ibid.

[20] Beasley-Murray, "The Christological Controversy," 6.

[21] Ibid.

[22] George Beasley-Murray, *Jesus and the Future: An Examination of the Criticism of the Eschatological Discourse, Mark 13, with Special Reference to the Little Apocalypse Theory* (London: Macmilllan & Co., 1954), 172.

[23] Ibid., 183.

[24] Ibid., 190.

[25] Ibid.

[26] Beasley-Murray, "The Christological Controversy," 2.

[27] Ibid., 6.

CHAPTER 10

Jesus and/as Parable of God

Constructing a Faith Image of Jesus

How can today's shaping of Jesus be faithful to Baptist insights into the Christian faith and at the same time be faithful to contemporary approaches to the study of the historical Jesus? How can we envision in our day the relationship between the Christ of faith and the Jesus of history, or how can we move back and forth from credulous creedal approaches, to critical historical approaches, to creative literary approaches—to post-modern and post-critical construal involving the competence and need of readers?

The work of two Baptist New Testament scholars provides some guidance in arriving at an answer to this question: the transplanted British scholar Norman Perrin and the American scholar Dan O. Via. These two scholars have been influential in critical approaches to the Gospels and the life of Jesus. But they have seen the limitations of historical approaches and the positive role of readers who construct faith-images of Jesus and are involved in the present-day revelation-event. Perrin offers advice on the question of the significance of historical knowledge of Jesus and his teaching.[1] Via suggests how "the recital of God's acts in the Bible, naively portrayed as historical" functions in the "revelation situation—primarily for the New Testament writers but by implication also for us." He is interested in the factors that compose the "actualization of revelation."[2]

Norman Perrin: Christian Proclamation and Faith Knowledge

Norman Perrin is, in part, a product of the British Baptist tradition and discusses the significance of knowledge of the historical Jesus and his teaching from the perspective of one who has been taught to "believe in Jesus."[3]

The major part of his work on *Rediscovering the Teaching of Jesus* is devoted to study of the parabolic teaching of Jesus. The final chapter deals with the question of the significance of this historical knowledge. Three different kinds of knowledge must be distinguished according to Perrin:

> First, there is the essentially descriptive historical knowledge of Jesus of Nazareth with which we have been concerned all through this book. Then, secondly, there are those aspects of this knowledge which, like aspects of historical knowledge of any figure from the past, can become significant to us in our present in various ways. Thirdly there is knowledge of Jesus of Nazareth which is significant only in the context of specifically Christian faith, i.e. knowledge of him of a kind dependent upon the acknowledgement of him as Lord and Christ.[4]

Perrin calls these three kinds of knowledge "historical knowledge," "historic knowledge," and "faith-knowledge." Historical knowledge exists independently of any specific interest in it or any usefulness ascribed to it. Historic knowledge depends upon the establishment of some point of contact between that knowledge from the past and the situation of humans in the present. Faith-knowledge becomes significant at the level of religious faith, belief, or commitment. Faith-knowledge may or may not be historical knowledge. That is, historical knowledge may come to provide the significance of faith-knowledge—but so can myth, legend, sage, or a combination of these.

Historical knowledge of Jesus could include Jesus' acceptance of his death as the consequence of his proclamation of the Kingdom and of his table fellowship with tax collectors and sinners. Historical knowledge under certain circumstances can become historic knowledge. That is, it can assume a direct significance for the present. The historical knowledge of Jesus' acceptance of the cross can become historic knowledge as it influences a future time touched and moved by it in some way. We move from historical knowledge to historic knowledge, then, as the event from the past assumes significance for future time. Faith-knowledge depends upon special worth being attributed to the person concerned so that that knowledge assumes a significance beyond the historic. The Christian confession, "Christ died for my sins in accordance with the scriptures," is a statement of faith. It is faith-knowledge, depending upon recognition of Jesus as the Christ the son of the living God.

Faith-knowledge of Jesus Christ arises in response to the challenge of the proclamation of the church. Each and all of the possible forms of proclamation can mediate the encounter of faith with the Christ present to faith in them. That is, the various forms of proclamation produce a "faith-image" of Jesus. The image mediated by the multiple forms of Christian proclamation is to be distinguished from the historical Jesus (even though the historical knowledge of Jesus may have been a factor in its creation). The ultimate origin of faith-knowledge is Christian proclamation—not historical research. The Greek word translated "preaching" or "proclamation" is kerygma. "God decided, through the foolishness of our proclamation [*kerygma*], to save those who believe" (1 Cor. 1:21).

> What gives this faith-image validity is the fact that it grows out of religious experience and is capable of mediating religious experience; that it develops in the context of the complex mixture of needs, etc., which originally created, and continues to create, an openness toward the kerygma; and that it can continue to develop to meet those needs.[5]

What is the relevance of historical knowledge of Jesus? Perrin emphasizes the role of historical knowledge in validating faith-images. He suggests that the challenge of distinguishing true faith-images from false faith-images is particularly strong in America where there is a multitude of conflicting and competing kerygmata. Everything from "radical right racism" to "revolutionary Christian humanism" is declared to be Christian proclamation. In light of this situation,

> We believe we have the right to appeal to our limited, but real, historical knowledge of Jesus. The true kerygmatic Christ, the justifiable faith-image, is that consistent with the historical Jesus. The significance of the historical Jesus for Christian faith is that knowledge of this Jesus may be used as a means of testing the claims of the Christs presented in the competing kerygmata to be Jesus Christ. To this limited extent our historical knowledge of Jesus validates the Christian kerygma; it does not validate it as kerygma, but it validates it as Christian.[6]

Perrin discusses the resources of the synoptic tradition understood in light of modern historical knowledge of Jesus ("a phenomenon necessarily absent from the New Testament"). There is a "complete and absolute identification, by the early Christians, of the earthly Jesus of Nazareth and the risen Lord of Christian experience."

> To early Christianity the Jesus who had spoken in Galilee and Judea was the Christ who was speaking through the prophets and in Christian experience. It is for this reason that we have the remarkable phenomenon of sayings of Jesus being treated as a part of general Christian instruction in the epistles . . . For this reason Paul can speak of words from the Lord and mean words possibly originating from Jesus but heavily reinterpreted in the church and overlaid with liturgical instructions . . . because he is completely indifferent as to whether all, some *or none* had, in fact, been spoken by the earthly Jesus.[7]

Perrin declares that we can go beyond the help that knowledge of the historical Jesus can be in providing control and acting as a check on false or inappropriate faith-images. Historical knowledge of Jesus can be directly relevant to faith.[8]

> If the believer in response to the kerygma stands in a relationship with God parallel to that in which a Galilean disciples stood in response to Jesus' proclamation of the Kingdom of God, which the synoptic Gospels necessarily claim, then teaching addressed to that latter situation is applicable to the former. In this way historical knowledge of the teaching of Jesus becomes directly applicable to the believer in any age.[9]

Dan O. Via: The Actualization of Revelation

In the history of the church's understanding of Jesus there was movement from a dogmatic Christ to a historical Jesus, with historical understandings correcting or modifying traditional dogmatic perspectives. Other elements become important. The end in mind becomes important. Praxis impinges upon the dogmatic/historical dialectic. For those approaching Jesus solely as a historical figure able to serve as a moral exemplar (for example, Socrates), the reconstruction of the historical personality of Jesus may be the focus—with this reconstruction able to impinge upon contemporary life. For those in the church, the practice of doctrine may be the end in mind, following Jesus as he reveals and actualizes a divine love, justice, and peace. Praxis has the capacity to focus and bring to satisfying completion the incomplete intellectual exercise involved in dogmatic and historical investigation.

When the contemporary reader recognizes the literary and poetic aspect of the evangelists and assumes the same sort of creative approach, the reader is close to being able to correlate the different sorts of knowledge involved in the Gospels and the study of Jesus. Dan Via has dealt with the revelation of God in the New Testament from a systematic perspective. Via takes statements of Paul in the first two chapters of 1 Thessalonians as paradigmatic in their emphasis on four elements:

1. the word of God or content
2. the power of the Holy Spirit
3. the way a particular situation influences the expression of the gospel
4. the place of human reception.

> Paul refers to the gospel (1:5; 2:4) or word of God (2:13) as rational content or *logos* (1:5 a) and as empowered by the Holy Spirit (1:5 b). He also speaks of the way in which the Thessalonians have received the gospel (1:6; 2:13) and of the historical circumstances in which he had worked and they had received the word (1:6; 2:2, 4-7, 14-17). These four factors recur regularly in the New Testament witnesses, although not with the same emphasis or degree of explicitness. My argument [is] that for the New Testament, revelation is actual only when all four elements are operative. Only the four together are sufficient.[10]

In his chapter on "Event and Word: The Historical Jesus," Via deals with the question of the relationship between historical actuality and revelation from the perspective of contemporary attitudes about history as human ways of creating meaning.[11] Via argues that historical actuality (as distinguished from linguistic representation) is in a certain way a necessary factor in the revelation situation. In the life process these two elements are dialogically interactive.

In light of the fact that revelation in the New Testament "is so materially constructed from theological intentions and imaginative decisions (to which we have access only through our own imaginative, theological, and theoretical decisions)," Via would reverse the normal connection between the event and language while maintaining the close relationship between the two:

> God reveals God's self in the language, the word, the text—language as the event of revelation—and the historical events narrated are a set of symbols for the event character of the word and for the capacity of the present situation to be a new redemptive event under the impact of the word.[12]

The claim that God is eschatologically active in the ministry of Jesus "is a theological affirmation derived from the faith experience or existential experience in which the merging of the Jesus tradition and one's present situation is experienced powerfully."[13] The story of the event and the event that is narrated itself have the same power—the power of revelation to liberate and transform.

There is, then, an ontological connection between the event and the story. The power of the narrative does not rest merely on its literary qualities. There is a dialogue between event and narrative but there is also a dialogue between the event/narrative, the imaginative reception and configuration of the word by human beings, and a historical-cultural situation in which the received word is meaningful.

Conclusion

Both Perrin and Via have concentrated upon Jesus' use of parables in their historical and theological writings. A creative and legitimate extension of the vehicle of parable enables us to appreciate not only Jesus' use of parables in the proclamation of the Kingdom but also Jesus as parable—as parabolic revelation of God. A Baptist concern with "believing in Jesus" may be illuminated by this extension—concern with the subject of belief (the contemporary believer) and the object of belief (the God of Jesus Christ). A literary or parabolic capacity is not a static quality. It involves a capacity to observe different levels of meaning, a narrative or story level whereby elements in the narrative fit together to tell a story, a more or less "literal" level whereby the text is referring to events in a real historical world and levels of significance beyond the story and literal level. Literary capacity involves the capacity to observe conventional poetic meanings involved in simile and metaphor, parable and story—meanings that are clearly intended and discerned by ancient authors and readers. But literary capacity involves moving beyond those conventional meanings to new meanings that are appropriate for contemporary readers.

A literary approach, then, will not be constrained by so-called original "intentions" of ancient authors. These intentions, as they may be discerned, will be seen as involved in the originating circumstances of the text. A literary approach to the life of Jesus may even come to be less concerned with Jesus' understanding of himself and/or our inability to prove scientifically some original self-understanding because Jesus' self-understanding would not be a final constraint upon Jesus' meaning and significance.

Approaching the Gospels and the life of Jesus from the perspective of narrative or story as well as from metaphysical or scientific historical perspectives allows us to map Jesus to the human historical situation where revelation takes place. It allows us to relocate doctrinal conceptions in the human faith-situation as interpretations of Jesus.

The Roman Catholic theologian Roger Haight has specified three ways that Jesus research (rediscovery of the Jesus of Nazareth) is affecting Christ research (Christology) in a new postmodern paradigm. What he says illuminates possibilities valid for traditions beginning with an emphasis upon believing in Jesus and in Jesus' divine status.

First, contemporary Jesus study reinforces the conviction that Jesus of Nazareth is the object of Christology. Second, Christology is affected through the reschooling of human imagination by means of the application of more direct historical images of Jesus. Unhistorical or purely dogmatic images are being called into question and historically viable construal of Jesus of Nazareth as the Christian mediator of God is offered. A third way that Jesus' research affects Christology has to do with the distinction between Jesus' intrinsic historical meaning and Jesus' later signification. Later interpretations of Jesus may capture reality even though they may not have been part of Jesus' understanding.[14] Jesus research and the reschooling of our imaging of Jesus become a way of recovering aspects of the mystery of God that were obscured by classical doctrines. Haight speaks of Jesus as a powerful and dialogical "symbol of God" for Christian faith.

> . . . Christian faith in God mediated by Jesus is at the same time an opening up of imagination in a way that allows Jesus to be the parable of God . . . [I]n existential

terms this means that Christians encounter God in Jesus
. . . [W]ithin this encounter Jesus reveals God, that is,
mediates God and makes God present in a more conscious,
intense, and personal way. Christian salvation consists in
the encounter with the saving God in and through Jesus,
so that Jesus saves by revealing and making God present.[15]

Satisfying shaping of Jesus today involves the shaping and reshaping of faith and imagination. Shaping of Jesus that satisfies Baptist faith and life is offered by a multifaceted and dialogical shaping of the object of faith and the subject of faith. The sacred is re-experienced as the word of the gospel is expressed and experienced in particular human and historical situations—in content and power.

Notes

[1]Norman Perrin, *Rediscovering the Teaching of Jesus* (New York and Evanston: Harper & Row, 1967), 207-48.

[2]Dan O. Via, *The Revelation of God and/as Human Reception in the New Testament* (Philadelphia: Trinity Press International, 1997), 38.

[3]Perrin, *Rediscovering*, 243.

[4]Ibid., 234.

[5]Ibid., 244.

[6]Ibid.

[7]Ibid., 245.

[8]Ibid., 246.

[9]Ibid., 247. Perrin remarks, "It is precisely for this reason . . . that some actual teaching of the earthly Jesus was taken up into the synoptic tradition, and that the very concept of a Jesus tradition came into being" (*Rediscovering*, 248).

[10]Via, *The Revelation of God*, 8-9.

[11]Ibid., 70-71.

[12]Ibid., 77.

[13]Ibid., 78.

[14]Roger Haight, *Jesus: Symbol of God* (Maryknoll, NY: Orbis Books, 1999), 36-39.

[15]Roger Haight, *The Future of Christology* (New York and London: Continuum, 2005), 49.

www.ingramcontent.com/pod-product-compliance
Lightning Source LLC
Chambersburg PA
CBHW071225160426
43196CB00012B/2416